DR BUCKE REVISITED

Cosmic Consciousness – Quantum Consciousness

Pearl Hawkins

ATHENA PRESS
LONDON

DR BUCKE REVISITED
Cosmic Consciousness – Quantum Consciousness
Copyright © Pearl Hawkins 2004

All Rights Reserved

ISBN 1 84401 222 0

First Published 2004 by
ATHENA PRESS
Queen's House, 2 Holly Road
Twickenham, TW1 4EG
United Kingdom

Printed for Athena Press

DR BUCKE REVISITED
Cosmic Consciousness – Quantum Consciousness

This book is dedicated to my grandchildren and to my brother Michael's grandchildren, Deniel, Hollie, Jodie, Aled, Rhys and any other grandchild that may issue after my day.

Acknowledgements

My sister-in-law sowed the seed. Veronica was looking for words of comfort after the death of my mother with whom I had had a pained relationship. 'You should write it all down.' Over a period of two decades that phrase haunted me.

I began writing. Very quickly, it was not my mother who emerged but my grandmother, Edith Walters. She became the founder member of the Church of Nazareth having become ostracised from her Baptist community. She was, in their terms, a heretic. I then chanced upon two books, which crystallised my sense of direction: *Cosmic Consciousness* by Dr Maurice Bucke and *The Gnostic Gospels* by Elaine Pagels. I had already become immersed in the fascinating world of quantum physics. A librarian, noting two regular visitors chasing the same titles, introduced me to Professor Jean Walters who expressed an interest in my project. Her experience in the cognitive sciences, sensitivity and encouragement was my safety net throughout the writing of this book. I am deeply indebted to Jean and the county librarian, Hazel James, for bringing us both together.

Survey 2003 generated a wealth of treasured personal accounts from people who took a leap of faith in a perfect stranger unattached to an institutional research body. I have been privileged to receive that trust and willingness to cooperate when I have needed clarification. I am grateful to each and every one.

Last, but not least, my deepest debt of gratitude goes to Alun, my husband, who has always been there for me, quietly supportive, loving and gentle, taking on trust my flights into obscure corners and making that journey all the more comfortable.

I am aware that much of what I have to say touches lightly upon issues that are properly subject for discussion in depth. However, my hope is that I have succeeded in making my perspective clear and in so doing created, as the Bishop of Durham once said, 'The right kind of disturbance.'

Foreword by Professor Jean Walters

Our librarian, who having noted that two people in the county library were reading the same titles, introduced Pearl and me to each other.

I was exploring my own project on human consciousness. We discovered we were travelling from opposite ends towards the same intellectual centre, both having recognised a concept called *'cosmic consciousness'* that enables mankind to be at one with the universe and with each other. Pearl had written her book but had realised that for its completion it needed contemporary accounts of spirituality.

I was overwhelmed by the breadth of knowledge that is contained in her work and the way it is put together to present a case for the existence of *cosmic consciousness*. Since having received a profound experience identical to that of Dr Bucke, Pearl decided to follow up his 1901 survey with Survey 2003. I am convinced that many people have experienced the total 'belongingness' that Pearl describes, but because it is purely a subjective experience it is difficult to explain to others. In her book, published 2004, she goes a long way to externalise this experience and make people aware of its deep significance. Once touched by such an event you are never the same again. As Pearl points out, it changes your whole perception of life.

Pearl maintains she is not an academic. I maintain

she should not apologise for that. She is not undertaking a scientific treatise but to identify something that is truly innate to all human beings but is barely recognised as such. With the assistance of respondents' submissions to Survey 2003, her writing promises to be a voyage of discovery in which we become aware of our Cosmic Conscious selves, and our existence as part and parcel of a Universal Whole.

Introduction

Cosmic consciousness, as its name implies, is a consciousness of the universe and our intimate link with creation. Recorded accounts of its *peak* intensity remain remarkably consistent throughout every age, e.g. from ancient Hinduism some three thousand years ago to modern times, as respondents to Survey 2003 demonstrate (Part Two). The prime purpose of Survey 2003 is to identify the varying intensities of *cosmic consciousness* using experiential accounts. Throughout our overview in Part One, we recognise *cosmic consciousness* as a heightened awareness arising from a high level of spirituality possessed by the individual.

All who experience *peak cosmic consciousness* find words are inadequate to express the wondrous power of universal love, yet each individual account is identifiably a *pcc* event. Recipients merge with a clear understanding of our cosmic link lodged firmly within human consciousness processes. Although *pcc* is a mystical experience of unity with a divine source of love, it is not supernatural; that is to say, it is not beyond the laws of nature. Received wisdom from the *pcc* event is that divinity and the natural laws of creation are indivisible, therefore this book is based upon the premise that the connective source of all intensities of *cc* – from that 'in my bones' feeling to its *peak* manifestation – is located somewhere in the human brain. As such, *cc* is open to neurobiological research.

It is also feasible that quantum physics may take more than a passing interest in *cc*, since consciousness is implicated in the behaviour of the particle in the atom. Whatever the level of interest science presently has in consciousness, it does not necessarily include a metaphysical dimension. However, should science one day discover factual evidence clearly identifying a spiritual faculty, such knowledge would inevitably influence the way we perceive ourselves. The implication for humankind is staggering. In Chapter Four we take an overview of science and its relevance to religion and spirituality in this modern age from a layman's perspective.

At the end of the nineteenth century, Dr Maurice Bucke, a psychiatrist, wrote his treatise entitled *Cosmic Consciousness*, consequent upon his own profound spiritual experience. Bucke's experience was, in fact, the *peak* intensity of *cc*, known throughout the world, variously, as Nirvana, Brahmic Splendour and Enlightenment, among other names. His book included a survey of *cc*, mostly from among his Canadian contemporaries. His treatise, which we consider in Chapter Three, was decidedly revolutionary for its time. Spirituality is seen not only as innate but as an evolving faculty, evolving since humankind became aware of spirituality, emerging at some point during pre-historic times.

Bucke's treatise is pivotal and timely. It turns us around to face head-on a scientific age. It disposes of supernatural concepts, effectively making divinity accessible to scientific investigation, a prospect to outrage if not to strike terror into the hearts and minds of good folk the world over. But we have nothing to fear from science except our fear of science. We have been given the capacity to climb into the driving seat and to stay there. If there is something to be discovered then it will be uncovered. It is an exciting prospect.

By choosing to recognise an innate spirituality synonymously and symbolically expressed in a myriad of ways within human love, which includes our relentless pursuit of truth, wisdom, and justice, we are confronted by its immediacy. Love is at once natural and divine, God is Love, and Love is God. Every language the world over has a word or many words to reflect spirituality when the simple word love could suffice. From the moment we are born love is so much a natural part of our experience we take it for granted. Without it our plight is dire and desperate, then it is all too conspicuous by its absence. So natural is love we are barely aware of its origin. Occasionally, we glimpse its source; enough to make the most hardened among us pause and reflect. At such moments spirituality reaches its *cosmic* dimension. Bucke saw that the development of spirituality in the individual is mirrored in its evolutionary growth through the ages. He believed *cc* would continue to evolve until it became the norm within the human psyche.

A *cc* event moves us out and away from our chosen frame of mind. *Cosmic consciousness* has the power to change perceptions, whether a believer in a chosen religion, atheist, agnostic or seemingly indifferent to 'God matters'; that is to say, secularised. Possibly for the first time we question some religious tenets, whilst at the same time, with fresh perspective, appreciate the truth and beauty that is to be found in sacred writings.

Cosmic consciousness informs and enlightens. We come to understand that there is a little more to life than we had realised. We are enabled to take charge of our own spirituality, our own gnosis, using the Greek definition of that word; knowledge gained intuitively. One can see at once how this direct route might seriously challenge some theological tenets. In Chapter Two we take a brief overview of the role gnostics have played since early AD centuries in keeping humankind 'grounded', keeping the individual in touch with his/her own spark of divinity. It has to be noted that Gnosticism was comprised of as many complex splinter groups, if not more so, than any orthodox religion. Therefore interest here is centred upon individuals who break through the edifice of convention to discover their own gnosis, their own *cosmic consciousness*.

This book begins (Chapter One) with a profile of one such individual; Edith Walters, a later day gnostic, though she would not have dreamt of using that label. Edith Walters was the author's grandmother, whose life was the original inspiration behind the writing of this book. Edith Walters became pastor of her own church at the beginning of the twentieth century having been fired and inspired by a religious revival that swept through Wales in 1904. She was a remarkable woman with a remarkable mission. This book places her in the public domain, but we wonder how many others throughout history died in obscurity having influenced their contemporaries by the driving force of *cosmic consciousness*, their individual gnosis.

Contents

Part One

Benjamin and Edith Walters, outside their home
at Ty Gwyn

Chapter One

Edith Walters 1876–1950

The Welsh Religious Revival of 1904 attracted headlines in the world's newspapers, devoting several columns and pictures to their reports.

People began to visit Wales from England, Norway, Germany, Russia, America and even Catholic countries such as France, Italy, Portugal, Spain and Ireland. Prayers were said for countries of the world. Places as far apart as India, China and Latin America would report powerful visitations.

(Abridged extracts from Eifion Evans:
The Welsh Revival of 1904)

The 1904 Revival was the last of several that had risen and abated intermittently throughout the nineteenth century. 1859 was a pinnacle, 1904 another. Edith Walters' life's work was a direct product of the 1904 spiritual awakening. Very few were unaffected by the fervour it generated as it raced through the Welsh landscape like fire through a forest in drought. Its message was immediate: the Holy Spirit is ignited from within. Individuals took command of their own gnosis, using that word in its purest sense to signify spiritual knowledge gained intuitively. In his book on the 1904 Welsh Revival, Eifion Evans tells how chapels ceased to have a schedule. They were never closed but always occupied by people offering personal witness and joining in rousing spontaneous congregational hymn singing, in full melodic harmony. Ministers came down from their pulpits. Hierarchies disappeared. Family quarrels were patched, enmities dissolved, marriages saved, generosity of spirit, tolerance and love reigned supreme. Exclamations of 'born again' and 'I've seen the light' were prolific. Pockets of mass hysteria were inevitable, but emerging out of this emotionally charged climate was evidence of profound events of *cosmic consciousness*, unchanged and unchanging from age to age up to the present day.

Edith Walters' *cosmic consciousness* would inform her life's work over the next five decades. She would become pastor of her own church. The 1904 Revival would have a profound influence upon Benjamin and Edith and their six girls. Benjamin was a man called upon to exercise unusual patience and devotion: he could not have dreamt of what he was about to take on when he married Edith, nee Price, at Saloam Chapel, Clydach, Llanelli Hill, Wales.

Edith Walters was a trained seamstress. She was an intelligent person who had received a good basic education for that time. Later she was to teach her husband to read and write. Benjamin's working life had begun at eight years old, underground in the coalmines. The Prices were – and still are – proud, ambitious, lively and talented. On the whole they continue to produce more than their fair share of teachers and preachers, social workers, lawyers and academics. When Edith showed signs of breaking away from her family's religious sphere, the Prices were filled with dismay by what they saw as Edith's retreat into mysticism. They eventually settled down, bemused but at all times tolerant and accepting. Her brother, Rev. Frederick Price, a missionary in China, tried several times to talk his sister around. She was not to be moved. He wanted to understand but he failed.

During the autumn of 1904 Edith Walters heard a voice from God (she always referred to the voice as 'Father') telling her to deliver a message to Evan Roberts, the leading revivalist of 1904. Prior to this she had experienced a profound spiritual event. Now a powerful force propelled her. She could not be dissuaded from paying a visit to Evan Roberts. A few weeks earlier she had given birth to her third child. For a young woman at the turn of the twentieth century a journey from Waunllapria, Brecon, to Aberystwyth, Mid Wales, was a huge undertaking. To the consternation of her family and her Baptist Church congregation, she set out leaving her two little girls, Violet and Evelyn, with family. She was not quite alone; baby Edna in need of her mother's milk had to go too.

To make contact with Evan Roberts Edith was obliged to enter a room full of men and make a public announcement. 'Father' had told her to come: she had a message to deliver. Evan Roberts was to lay aside his theological books and allow the Holy Spirit to be his guide. Interestingly, in Eifion Evans' account he refers to Roberts' agonising over whether, at that time, he should go back to his theological studies. Evan Roberts did not go back to college, but Eifion Evans does not say what influenced his final decision.

Soon after this event Benjamin and Edith came

south and finally settled in Brynna, which was then a tiny village near Cardiff City. Meetings were held in the house. The fact that there was religious activity in the home was not the least bit unusual for the times. People everywhere were doing the same thing. Moved by the Holy Spirit, spontaneous gatherings had become a necessary way of life. People met in makeshift tents, they gathered in open-air meetings near public houses, fairgrounds, market squares and at the work place. Miners met early underground, before their shift began, for prayer and personal witness. One hundred years later one can still hear echoes of that original fervour whenever the Welsh gather in a festival of hymn singing.

Those early meetings in the home degenerated into a noisy Tower of Babel. People came and 'talked in tongues'. Again, this was not so unusual; there was a frenzied fringe that was generated during excesses of religious emotion. Edith Walters quickly established control and the house meetings settled into a coherent form. It was at this juncture that Edith Walters finally became ostracised from her former Baptist community. 'Father' now told her to proclaim herself pastor of a church in embryo. The tenets of Baptism embrace personal salvation. Even so, Edith Walter's self-confessed experience of Christ having risen in her was altogether too challenging. Like the true gnostic she was, she professed to be in possession of her own individual gnosis. Her knowledge was gained by direct divine intervention, therefore she was now a heretic. She was accused of preaching a new doctrine, although, in fact, it was as old as the hills, stripped of supernatural elements and not a theological construct in sight. This, she proclaimed, was how it was when Christ walked on earth before events became confused by time, memory and imagination. Long after the embers of the Revival had died away in 1905/6, meetings held in Edith's home were to continue before transferring to a purpose-built church in Gelli Fedi Road, Brynna in 1924: the Church of Nazareth. It was dismantled in 1972. Not a trace remains.

Today, anyone wishing to know what special insight Edith Walters received in 1904 need only read what Reverend David Jenkins, Bishop of Durham, said in 1984. The Bishop confronts the inconsistencies that must arise between one language and another in translation and explores their impact upon our understanding of the scriptures. For example, the word 'virgin', he notes, is an unfortunate choice in the translation process, since it gave rise to a supernatural tale. The historicity of the resurrection story is also scrutinised and found wanting. Although his views created a furore, David Jenkins nevertheless survived to remain in the Anglican Church. He had said what many others had thought. The Bishop is undeterred; his faith unshaken. He feels *Free to Believe* (the title of his book) in a spiritual interpretation of Christ's birth and sees resurrection as a fact of our daily lives. Whereas he arrived at these conclusions through scholarship and rational thought, by careful study of the Holy Scriptures in their original Greek and Hebrew, Edith Walters arrived via divine revelation. It became a crusade, a route fraught with danger and pitfalls, but one that for her there was no choice but to follow.

Did she know she was one of many to reject a literal interpretation of the Bible, such as the father of Unitarianism Martin Cellarius (1499–1564, Strasbourg) and its later exponent in England, John Biddle (1615–1662)? In all probability these two men would have embodied their doctrine, preaching with authority, as did Edith Walters. There are many like examples throughout history. Did she know that ancient gnostics soon after the time of Christ had also challenged established orthodoxy in the same way? Probably not. Whether or not she had access to reference books and libraries that might have informed her is irrelevant since 'Father' had instructed her to set aside all books on theology except the Bible. God was to be the font of all knowledge. The voice in her head was the voice of Divinity. 'Father' governed her whole existence. In the light of her mission she was now the vehicle by which others would come to the new (old) doctrine. It was a mammoth move to make on the part of an individual, especially for a woman at that time.

All this while Edith was a thrifty, efficient housewife and mother of six girls: Violet, Evelyn, Edna, Phyllis, Priscilla and Myrtle. For the first four, in those early years, life was not easy, being overlaid with a significant degree of social isolation within the community, regarded as aloof and a 'cut above the rest', it was difficult and bewildering for little girls to find themselves cast in this role. There are stories of them always having to be well turned out, hair beribboned, petticoats and aprons starched to perfection, legging boots shiny black. All had good, clear skin and beautiful ringletted hair: jet black, light

auburn, titian and one deep rich auburn. By all
accounts they were a sight to behold. Fortunately,
Edith Walters was blessed with a devoted husband. He
accepted his wife's work, but he did not become an
adherent of her Church. His daughters would tell how
their father would scrub floors, black-lead the fire
range, polish the brass, wash nappies and so on,
carefully locking all doors first in case the neighbours
should catch sight of him doing such unmanly tasks.
In every way he was a supportive husband. He was also
a strict but loving father. The girls knew exactly what
was expected of them from both parents.

Benjamin was a self-employed 'headings' man
working on contract to Brynna Wood Mines and other
collieries in the area. The task of his men was to drive
headings through the rock face to open up coal seams.
During the prosperous years the family enjoyed a high
standard of living and the home reflected this.
Consequently, theirs was not the typical humble home
found in their tiny village. This too caused difficulties
in a small, introspective community, and was
undoubtedly compounded by Edith Walters' natural
reticence; she was given to keeping her own counsel.
Whilst quietly friendly, she was not a free, out-going
mixer.

Even so, she would marshal one or two of her girls,
each bearing a basket of garden produce – all grown in
their large garden – fruit and vegetables, together with
eggs, freshly baked bread and sometimes meat from
their pigs and chickens. Off she would go once a week
to visit women in a neighbouring village whose
husbands drank or gambled away the family's meagre

income. In those lean years women often went undernourished and were weakened by childbearing. One of the baskets contained soap, de-lousing agent, clean towels and a change of underclothes freshly laundered from the previous visit. Rolling up her sleeves, Edith bathed the children in a tin bath, in front of a fire, if there was one.

Later, the family faced a degree of poverty themselves when Benjamin became semi invalid, suffering silicosis from the fine silica particles settled in the lungs, the symptoms of which were all too familiar among the miners of the South Wales coalfields. Silicosis was not a recognised disease then. Even as late as 1936 there would be little help for people unable to earn a living. The Unemployment Assistance Board created in 1934 offered meagre help grudgingly given. Edith and Ben Walters were lucky. Their poverty was relative. They were almost self sufficient in food production. Friends tilled the soil; seeds were sown the following year, clothes made from cheap remnants. Mending, darning and patching were important activities. The emphasis was on thrift and innovation. There was also a fair-sized nest egg too. Benjamin Walters had earned good money in his working years.

Edith Walters was able to continue her ministry practically unimpeded by circumstances. There was even enough money to buy land and build a church, the Church of Nazareth. This was a time, in the early twentieth century, when traditional theology was still reeling from Darwin's *Origin of the Species* (1859) and his *Decent of Man* (1871). They were turbulent, challenging times for Christianity. Whilst these works presented a direct confrontation between science and religion, the mere suggestion that spiritual insights might too have evolved through the ages, rising above literal interpretation of the Bible was – and still is – anathema to the whole of Christendom. What distinguished Edith Walters from most others was that she embodied her spiritual interpretation of the Bible. She set out to practise what she preached. The spiritual birth of Christ had arisen in *her*. The living spirit of Christ was in *her*. *She* became the embodiment of the resurrected Christ. No less. Strong meat indeed; small wonder her close followers would number little over a dozen at any given time. Edith Walters held the essence of a perfume too strong to inhale. Many could not bear it and turned away, others stayed to remain faithful throughout her forty-six-year ministry.

Those who came to visit expecting to discover some strangeness of character or disposition went away disappointed. Here was a woman who professed to be guided and governed by a divine presence, yet her sanity could not be held in doubt. She was a perfectly rational and practical-minded person. There was about her an arresting presence and a quiet, charismatic authority but she did not seek to dominate. She was not known to engage in contentious argument or give advice, yet somehow she didn't need to since she lived entirely by example. She was more given to asking the pertinent question, leaving the individual to sort out the answer. There was no hint of naivety about her. One sensed, too, that she was a shrewd judge of character.

Edith Walters' time was devoted to her children and

her ministry. She did not set out to evangelise. People came to her from far and wide. She made no attempt to raise her own profile, on the contrary she was gentle and self-effacing. Yet, when she stood in the pulpit she was transformed into a magnetic personality possessing great authority. She did not raise her voice or gesticulate. She was innocent of standard techniques used in oratory to whip up passions and stir emotions. What she had to say was said very simply, delivered with intense inner conviction and absolute sincerity. There was no preparatory work, no written sermons. She preached spontaneously, the Holy Spirit her guide at all times. The congregation too was governed by spontaneity in its hymn singing, personal witness and readings.

Imagine for a moment this small-framed lady rising from her seat in the pulpit, standing waiting, silently looking at each and every person in turn sitting in the pews, and then in quiet but arresting tones begin to read, for example:

> Believest thou not that I am in the Father, and the Father in me? The words that I speak unto you I speak not myself; but the Father that dwelleth in me, he doeth the work.

> St John, 14:11

As she spoke, 2,000 years rolled away. The spirit of Christ was speaking directly to those present. A reading might be enough. At other times it would be followed by an interpretation. The poetry of the Bible had a simple meaning: Jesus was an advanced soul who came among us to save us from indifference and encourage a belief in an inner spiritual calling. When Edith Walters spoke there was a clear implication that she too was an advanced soul whose mission also was to remind us that the birth of Christ symbolised the awakening of our soul, Christ in us.

More controversially, Edith Walters taught that Jesus of Nazareth was the natural-born child of Mary and Joseph. Christ was not the only begotten Son of God. The word 'only' is challenged. God was not to be limited. There are many Sons and Daughters of God, some more advanced than others. Jesus Christ was the leading light in the world. Human beings wrote the Bible, and as such it is an imperfect record, its spiritual message more potent and meaningful than its historical authenticity or supernatural accounts. With every utterance she exuded the powerful authority of the 'Living Christ'. She was the instrument through which 'Father' spoke to his children, as Christ had been before her. In times past Edith Walters would have been burned at the stake for saying a lot less.

One Sunday Rev. Price visited his sister's church, where he gave an interesting and graphic account of the Baptist Christian Mission among the people of China. Although there was nothing remotely arrogant about Fred Price, he nevertheless adhered to the current view of the time: that all foreign, non-Christian cultures were primitive and, therefore, needed to be rescued from their unenlightened ways. The love Rev. Price bore for the Chinese people was plainly evident, but though he held their ancient culture in the highest regard it did not shake his belief that their need was for conversion into the one and only true faith.

When he had done, his sister raised herself from her seat in the pulpit and for several seconds stood in silence before delivering 'Father's' message quietly and simply. In essence she told those present that the 'heathen' was to be found within us all; it was not for us to presume God's children were confined to national boundaries or religious beliefs. His Holy Spirit was free to move across the world unfettered. We are all God's children. The Kingdom of Heaven comes to all who would believe, irrespective of persons or nationalities, creeds and cultures. *God moves in mysterious ways His wonders to perform... In my Father's house are many mansions...* Doubtless brother Fred knew his sister's views but in all probability had not expected a public declaration. This was a clear rebuke to his life's work. He accepted it with dignity, as one had learned to expect from this highly-respected man. It was clear that what Edith Walters had been called upon to say had cost her dearly, though she would have known that the close bond between them could not be breached.

Edith Walters almost certainly experienced her enlightenment during her early twenties. Regrettably, we do not have her first-hand account of it in full, and those who might have heard it are no longer alive. It is known that she constantly proclaimed that she had been 'born again', risen in Christ. She spoke of 'light' indescribable. She referred frequently to the 'heavens opening', of unutterable 'joy and love', and 'knowing' that she had been chosen to do God's work. In fact there were frequent allusions to what we now recognise as the peak of *cosmic consciousness*. (This same event is illustrated in Survey 2003.) All this would be stated only from the pulpit. She did not preach or talk 'religion' when out of it. Retrospectively then, and realistically, we can be reasonably sure Edith Walters was initiated by a *peak cosmic consciousness* experience. In fact, she lived in a continuous cosmic dimension. It conditioned her whole consciousness throughout her life's mission. There were rare times during her ministry when *cosmic consciousness* deserted her and she would be plunged into silences lasting for days at a time. During her mute periods she felt deserted and forsaken, but accepted them with patience. However, onlookers sensed her suffering. She lived in complete obedience to the voice inside her and frequently referred to 'visitations' and 'revelations'. Even so, dedicated as she was to her calling, those close to her knew of her frailties and human vulnerability. She was not the archetypal saint. The spirit was perfect, the human being was not.

Edith Walters died leaving no writings of consequence behind. Her daughters were distraught to discover she had destroyed her many poems and written work soon after her husband's death, saying simply that they were not good enough. One pocket 1949 Diary was found which contains sparse, cryptic entries. There is one heartrending entry:

> Sobbed in pulpit could not go on for a little while, then I spoke on...

At very low ebb, she had already begun her journey into cancer and an agonising death. Pain management at that time was wholly inadequate That last year of her life was marked by long silent periods of retreat, perhaps mute for up to a week at a time in:

Obedience to 'Father's' will.

Her daughters, with infinite love and tenderness, nursed her at home. Her suffering and courage were unforgettable.

Following her death in 1950, Edith's followers were grief-stricken and moribund, unable to see a way forward. Onlookers were dismayed to witness a subtle transformation taking place. Gradually, 'Our Pastor' became the object of worship in exactly the way people pray to Christ or the Virgin Mary. She had become their God. Ancient history was repeating itself in microcosm. Their reaction confirmed what had hitherto been suspected; the faithful few had adored, almost worshipped their pastor in her lifetime. At times it had been a depressing spectacle. She so clearly had not wished to be placed on a pedestal. Now that her restraining influence was gone her followers were rudderless. Without her physical presence how were they to deal with 'Christ in us'? They did not know. They had been too close. They had not really understood her message. This was the awful truth. Edith Walters' teaching had been inwardly directed towards that spark of divinity within us all; the Holy Bible distilled into a spiritual interpretation. She had taught her followers to look within, take responsibility for their own spiritual journey and turn no man or woman into God.

As her eldest granddaughter I had been an intermittent visitor to the Church of Nazareth during my teenage years. Now, witnessing how the vacuum created by her death was being filled, I left the church, but I was troubled because I felt compelled to return to reiterate the pastor's central message in a church service – 'turn no man or woman into a god'. I eventually did return. The reaction was one of incomprehension. Those loyal and faithful few were nonplussed and a touch patronising, but just as affectionate as always. I left the church for the second time but could not walk away from the questions that remained unanswered. Edith Walters' life had to mean something. Surely it couldn't just end here? Surely she had not gone through all that to no purpose? I became acutely aware of how desperately alone my grandmother must have felt. The pastor had known of her followers' love, loyalty and blind faith, but she must also have known that they did not truly understand. She had died with that knowledge. That was her cross. As a teenager I had had more important things to think about. Now at age twenty there was a dawning, heartbreaking realisation of how lonely her life had been. What did it all mean? Why had there been no one to offer her spiritual consolation in her last days?

Over the next few years I wrestled with the riddle of my grandmother's life. My quest to understand 'the pastor' eventually led to a complete acceptance of her life, mission and message, culminating in my own *peak* of *cosmic consciousness* event whilst out walking in our village. Nothing had prepared me for the magnitude of that event. A visit was made to the Church of Nazareth to share my experience. Not surprisingly perhaps, it fell on deaf ears. (Survey 2003 shows how unbelievable *peak cosmic consciousness* is to those who have not experienced it). No one was to tell me of the pastor's *peak* of *cosmic consciousness*. Retrospectively, I fear they could think only of their beloved pastor. I left the church for the third and last time.

The life of Edith Walters was extraordinary to say the least. Certainly it was sacrificial. She was an immensely strong character, basically a loner, a self-actualising person bonded to her calling: a life full of grace and quiet charm infused with tenacious determination. All who knew her were privileged to have lived within the orbit of her influence.

★

The aftermath of Dr Maurice Bucke's *peak* of *cosmic consciousness* (subject of an overview in Chapter Three) brought about an intellectual treatise followed by his survey. Both are worthy of unprejudiced consideration. Bucke recognises spirituality as an evolving faculty in the human species. The peak of human consciousness, manifestly cosmic in character, has surfaced from time immemorial, recorded in the annals of history, notably among founder members of the world's great religions and among lesser-known individuals, as the life of Edith Walters demonstrates. Bucke considered this evolving faculty is exposed to genetic and environmental influences and is becoming more and more prevalent in world populations, but before attempting an outline of Bucke's treatise we should acknowledge the part played by individuals in past times faced with their own gnosis; *cosmic consciousness.*

Bucke died at the turn of the century, just as Edith Walters was about to embark upon her gnostic journey. In the next chapter we take an overview of those early gnostics who were profoundly influenced by Jesus of Nazareth, himself a gnostic of supreme magnitude, and take a look at the hidden role Gnosticism has played in leavening the bread of spiritual nourishment throughout the centuries.

★

Chapter Two

An Overview

The Poet

I sent my soul through the invisible
Some letter of the After Life to spell
And after many days my soul return'd
And said, 'Behold, myself am Heav'n and Hell'

The Rubaiyat of Omar Khay yam

THE GNOSTICS

We know Gnosticism was practised well before the Christian era. Gnostics' ideas were a melting pot of influences drawn from Asia, Babylonia, Syria, Greece and Egypt. During the early AD centuries gnostics were known to infiltrate mainstream Christian groups, exerting their influence from within until they were expelled. By the second century there were as many thriving gnostic sects as there were hundreds of Christian splinter groups. In general, gnostic Christian sects absorbed Christ's spiritual message into their own mythologies. Conversely, Christianity built a theology around the historical Jesus, the life and times of Jesus, which incorporated the notion of a child born of a virgin and a literal bodily resurrection. Gnostics took the opposite view. Some believed Christ's resurrection occurred at the moment of death when the spirit was released, whilst others saw clearly that the resurrection was symbolic of a personal spiritual encounter. Most were firm in their assertion that Jesus was the natural son of Joseph.

One can almost visualise hands raised in horror if not repulsion at the mere mention of Gnosticism. Gnosticism has had an extremely bad press over the centuries, especially from within the Christian faith, and not without reason. It was a contaminant during the early development of Christian theology around the second century AD.

Several of the very many gnostic sects were decidedly anti-Christian. Collectively, a maelstrom of ideas was cast into belief systems, elements of which were darkly repressive. Yet within that maelstrom we detect kernels of purity and truth, *cosmic consciousness* linking the minds of man with creation, with his universe. Ancient history offers tantalising glimpses into what times were truly like, which is all the more reason for unprejudiced approaches.   New archaeological finds add to an evaluation of evolving religious progression.

One such landmark of historical importance took place in the mid twentieth century. This was the discovery of ancient parchments at Nag Hammadi, some of which seriously challenge biblical interpretation. These were Coptic translations written on datable papyrus 350–400 AD, but scholarly estimates about when some of the original texts were written range from 50–180 AD. The Nag Hammadi codices are not to be confused with the Dead Sea Scrolls discovered about the same time, although both are important in the study of the origins of Christianity. Some claim the

Nag Hammadi finds reveal more about the early Christian development than do the Dead Sea Scrolls.

The parchments were found by one Muhammad Ali al-Samman whilst digging for fertilised soil among the mountain caves near Nag Hammadi in Upper Egypt. There he discovered a metre-high earthenware jar which he smashed, hoping it might contain gold. He was disappointed. He took home some loose papyrus and thirteen leather-bound papyrus books, dumping them next to the oven. His mother thought they would come in handy for kindling the fire. Several papyrus leaves were in fact burnt or lost. Fortunately for posterity, Raghib, a local teacher, suspected their value, and so began a long and tortuous journey from obscurity to where these precious writings are now, under the auspices of UNESCO, scattered among the world's scholars so that no nation can claim monopoly of possession. Muhammad Ali al-Samman had indeed found gold.

Among the thirteen codices found are the Apocryphon of John, Gospel of Thomas, Secret Book of James, The Gospel of Philip, the Letters of Peter to Philip, The Gospel of Truth, Apocalypse of Peter, the Gospel to the Egyptians and Hypostasis of the Archons.

Research on the Nag Hammadi codices reveals remarkable insight into the early post Christ era. It seriously challenges the actual bodily resurrection of Christ and his physical birth born of a virgin. As translations percolate into public domain they may herald shifts in Christian thinking from the grass roots up, if not among the more die-hard in theological circles. They are likely to bring controversy and pain to traditionalists and considerable relief to struggling believers.

Permeating the Nag Hammadi Gospels is a clear understanding of *cosmic consciousness*, the very same spiritual insight upon which Dr Maurice Bucke based his treatise written a hundred years ago, the very same spiritual insight taught by Edith Walters in Wales in the twentieth century, and the very same spiritual insight consistent with that found in Survey 2003. It is the same spiritual insight that has inspired artists, writers, poets and ordinary men and women throughout the ages. *Cosmic consciousness* can be viewed as the leaven in the bread, the rising spirituality open to all people inside or outside religious belief systems. Gnostics possess an intuitive knowing that is found to be threatening to orthodoxy, since they challenge the accepted interpretation of Christ's teaching. Gnostics were viewed as heretic then and still are today. From the gnostic perspective the reverse is true; it is orthodoxy that is heretical.

Before the discovery at Nag Hammadi, the presence of Gnosticism at that time was known to us mainly by default via the writings of Bishop Iranaeus, Ignatius and other protagonists of the early orthodox Church of Rome. They were troubled by the infiltration of gnostic perception into their midst. Gnostic writings were confiscated and burnt. Consequently, we have known little of the scale of their influence until an account was unearthed in 1945. The little that survived at Nag Hammadi offers only a tiny window onto the landscape that surrounded Christ's brief walk on earth.

Prof. Elaine Pagels, in her highly readable book *The Gnostic Gospels* spells out the subtleties between gnostic and Christian teachings that went undetected by many Christian followers. Iranaeus, disturbed by his contemporary, Valentinus, a poet and gnostic teacher and therefore a heretic, complained that Valentinians publicly confessed faith in one God but in private accuse Christians of mistaking images of God for reality that could not compare with Jesus' teaching that 'God is spirit'. The crucial difference between gnostics and the orthodox Christianity is one of spiritual authority. For Christianity that authority has been delegated by God to the church hierarchy and finally to the Son of God. Valentinian Gnosticism sees spiritual authority resting within the individual: *the Kingdom of God is within you*. It is not enough to believe, simply, in the Son of God.

It is as well to remember that early gnostic movements were as proliferate, complex and diverse as Christian sects. Some gnostic writings expound imaginative cosmic belief systems that rival anything found in Greek mythology. It is unfortunate that the Greek word 'gnosis' is used to label some of the earlier gnostic sects, since they could not legitimately claim pure insight into 'spiritual knowledge intuitively gained'. As is the case in many religious movements, Gnosticism too has its dark satanic underbelly. Its Demiurge is an arrogant, incompetent god born of a virgin. This lower god created the earth and all its lower life forms. In fact, he is a god of the same ilk mirrored in the Old Testament, arrogant, vengeful, jealous, cruel, prone to genocide, inflicting punishments upon his disobedient subjects.

Interestingly, Christians too introduced the idea of a virgin birth, but the Christian virgin brought forth a perfect being, a God in the image of man; a God of Love, compassion and unity; a God totally opposite to the Demiurge of Gnosticism. In retaining the idea of a virgin birth, Christianity turned aside from the metaphoric use of the divine Father and the divine Mother found in some gnostic writings. The New Testament does not relegate the virgin birth to myth and legend, neither is it merely a theoretical concept. New Testament writings go one step further, in the Resurrection story one finds categorical 'evidence' that Jesus the Christ was always God walking among us in the flesh. What is more, these are his quoted words. Following the crucifixion Jesus broke bread with his disciples:

> Behold my hands and feet that it is myself; handle me. And see; for a spirit hath not flesh and bones, as you see me have. And when he had thus spoken, he shewed his hands and feet. And while they believed not for joy, and wondered, he said unto them, 'Have ye here any meat?' And they gave him a piece of broiled fish, and of an honeycomb. And he took it, and did eat before them.
>
> St Luke, 24:39–43

How easily this can be accepted as a literal interpretation of a physical resurrection in preference to an assertion of the spirit risen in the flesh. The difficulty inherent in translating ancient script in evolving belief systems and how they overlap and influence each other is a fascinating subject about which scholars have written extensively. In addition, as we have noted, ancient findings such as the Nag Hammadi parchments provide brief flashes of insight. When all is said and done it appears we have little option but to admit that though we may not have all the answers, we should be prepared to move on as we become more enlightened. But for Christianity, as it was expounded by early scribes, dualistic in character – God, creator of creation, two separate entities – the options are seriously curtailed. So deep is the profound gulf between duality and the Oneness of creation, God and creation indivisible, it is unsurprising that some gnostic sects and Christianity were as incompatible then in those early AD centuries as Gnosticism and orthodoxy are today.

Of interest here are those gnostic writings that sing from the same song sheet, having the feel of spirituality gained naturally, springing from an unchanging, eternal font of knowledge. It is those gnostic sects, in addition to individual witnesses claiming internalised knowledge, that posed the deepest threat to the bewildering array of Christian sects vying for dominance in those early post-Christian centuries. Why were gnostics not more assertive? Why did they ultimately allow themselves to be overtaken by ambitious, competitive elements? One can be sure that they knew, as true gnostics of every age have always known, that confrontation was unnecessary.

The Nag Hammadi gnostic *Gospel of Philip*, entry No.16, has this to say on the subject:

> The authorities think that by their own power and volition they are accomplishing what they do. Yet the Holy Spirit in secret was energizing everything thru them as she wished. [Many Gnostic movements expressed The Holy Spirit/Ghost in the feminine gender.]

GNOSTICISM ANCIENT AND MODERN

Many gnostic sects and monotheist world religions have their roots in the *peak cosmic conscious* encounter of its founder member. Accounts of Jesus' teaching in the temple as a boy tell us that here was a child who at birth was possessed of a high degree of spirituality, possibly the most advanced soul the world has witnessed. His actual *peak* of *cosmic consciousness* is recorded in the four Gospels but appears the least distorted Matthew 3: 16

The Jewish priesthood at that time was corrupt and living in luxury whilst the mentally and physically sick, the handicapped, the poor, the frail, were seen as unclean, the outcasts. Jesus was their champion and, therefore, an outcast himself. He was a heretic from Jewish fundamentalism, a free thinker, a rebel, a highly controversial figure and a man with a unique revolutionary doctrine of love; on every count, a gnostic. Above all, he had a message for us all – we too could be born of the same spirit which he possessed. 'Love ye one another' was the only sensible, workable doctrine for the survival of human beings on earth.

Accepting the purest and simplest definition of a gnostic as one in possession of esoteric spiritual knowledge, Survey 2003 demonstrates that Gnosticism is as alive in the third millennium as ever it was in the first. We cannot begin to imagine how many solitary gnostics passed through the intervening two millenniums, neither can the full extent be known of those who attracted a following. History is littered with individuals having this special esoteric knowledge with a mission to bring understanding of our spirituality closer to home. Some household names spring to mind: Martin Luther (1483–1546), who challenged the Catholic belief in transubstantiation – the Catholic-held belief that bread and wine literally transformed into the flesh and blood of Christ; and George Fox (1624–91), founder member of the Quaker movement. Possibly each country has its own list of gnostics known in local history. In Wales Evan Roberts is well-known as a leader of the 1904 Revival. Edith Walters spent her forty-six-year ministry totally oblivious to the fact that her teachings echoed the same spiritual message found at Nag Hammadi in 1945 on parchment dated as early as 200 AD. It would appear many live and die without recognition, yet all essentially carry the same message: that we are responsible for our own spark of divinity.

Gnosticism is as widespread as the traditional movement from which their founder members depart as heretics. They are located in history from a broad spectrum of cultural sources. The Nag Hammadi cache illustrates this. Some writings were pagan in character and, as we have noted, cannot be classified as gnostic. Some are covertly Christian. Many, we are told, may have been influenced by Eastern mysticism, and others sprang from Jewish tradition, so that one can easily see how Gnosticism could be viewed as a reactive movement against the constraints of orthodox religions, but this would be an over simplification. Gnostics, characteristically, were known for their tolerance of other belief systems and each other. Sexual morality varied between groups, some advocating celibacy, others free love, whilst others were conventional. They resisted the authoritative dominance inherent in traditional hierarchical structures by rotating the leadership roles in their own. Along with priests (*temporarius*) women were accepted as priestesses, their writings valued equally with their male counterparts. Gender equality was further anathema to orthodoxy that felt undermined by gnosticism. It was traditional 'proof' of their heresy. To this day, orthodoxy continues to wrestle with itself on the matter of spiritual equality between men and women.

Understandably, since gnostics were claiming esoteric spiritual knowledge they were a threatening presence during the first three centuries, and particularly so when the traditional Church of Rome began to take root. Around the fourth century Gnosticism appeared to have disappeared leaving the ground clear for the giants of orthodox Christianity to crusade, evangelise, fight, thrive and flourish throughout succeeding centuries. Pagels makes a powerful case for the doctrine of the bodily resurrection having been used as a political expedient in early AD. Those who saw Christ literally in the flesh after the grave were in an unassailable position. In their witness lay legitimate claim that has authorised apostolic succession to this day. Each successive Pope traces his authority back to Peter, who is meant to be the first to witness the bodily resurrection of Christ. This in spite of Matthew and Luke's assertion in the New Testament that it was in fact Mary Magdalene who first 'saw' the risen Christ, a claim that for obvious reasons traditionalists would have found impossible to absorb. So a feminine supremacy was painted out.

For gnostics throughout all ages, male or female, the matter is a simple one. The resurrection is a reality: the metaphoric stone assuredly rolled away and Christ most assuredly rose in spirit, an event that is synonymous with *cosmic consciousness*. It is no small coincidence that respondents of Survey 2003 who have experienced *cosmic consciousness* reveal an independence of perspective on traditional Christian orthodoxy whilst remaining totally responsive to its core spiritual values. Being in possession of one's gnosis is to have come home. To this day, gnostics would say they are not obscure offshoots of Christianity but that Christianity is a religion rooted in and vaguely based on Gnosticism.

Our survey demonstrates that Gnosticism is not a vanquished Christian heresy. Carl Gustav Jung pays tribute to the intellectual expression of Gnosticism as:

Vastly superior to orthodox Christianity... which in the light of our present mental development has not lost but considerably gained in value.

In his *Psychological Types*, Jung's running theme centres on institutionalised Christianity having suffered grievously because of its suppression of spiritual spontaneity. Some might say that that grievous suffering is terminal. Gnostics would say that is not possible: our innate spirituality will find its own alchemy.

STEPPING STONES

Dostoyevsky, a gnostic himself and incisive commentator on the human soul, has this to say in his *Grand Inquisitor*:

Oh, Thou didst know that thy deed would be recorded in books, would be handed down to remote times and utmost ends of the earth, and thou didst hope that man, following Thee, would cling to God and not ask for miracles. But Thou didst know when man rejects miracles he rejects God too; for man seeks not so much God as the miraculous. And as man cannot bear to be without the miraculous, he will create new miracles of his own for himself, and will worship deeds of sorcery and witchcraft, though he might be a hundred times over a rebel, heretic and infidel.

And again:

There are three powers, three powers alone, able to conquer and to hold captive forever the conscience of impotent rebels for their happiness – those forces are miracles, mystery and authority. Thou hast rejected all three and hast set the example for doing so.

(The Brothers Karamazov: *The Grand Inquisitor*)

Religion is in essence the finite recognition of the infinite. Perhaps the purity and direction of that original enlightenment, *cosmic consciousness*, will continue to be preserved in collective imagery of miracle, mystery and authority for some time to come; miracle, mystery and authority – gold, frankincense and myrrh: humanity's gift to our God. Historically, miracle, mystery and authority endowed the Church with powerful tools of influence. They remain the potent forces of control in many of the world's religious communities. Miracle and mystery appeal to our imagination. They speak the language of emotion. Authority supplies our need for security and recognisable boundaries. Could the bridge of faith have survived without the powerful symbolism of love enshrined in the mystery of miracle, mystery and authority?

In spite of intolerance, bigotry, fanaticism and unspeakable deeds of cruelty perpetrated in the name of God, one can trace the thread of purpose running through the course of history. Love, the most powerful force on earth, triumphs whatever the obstacles. One cannot imagine how much more impoverished the world would be without art, music, literature and architecture inspired by the world's great religions to say nothing of the selfless lives and benevolent works performed by believers.

Cosmic consciousness brings with it a profound sense of affinity with others in a religious community.

Though acutely aware of the solid lid of theology, one feels at home with human beings responding to spiritual need. It is a profoundly moving experience to sit with others in any denominational setting, be it Catholic, Hot Gospel, Anglican, Greek Orthodox, knowing that we are all fellow travellers on the same path. As to the pain of divisive religious intolerance, all peace-loving people share this from outside and inside the Church. Although *cosmic conscious* people cannot defer to the authority implicit in the Church hierarchy, each soul being answerable to the divine spark within, it is perfectly understood how mediation, when administered by a spiritually-gifted priest, can become a stepping stone. Neither is this meant to suggest *cosmic conscious* people would not benefit from communion with others, quite the contrary. The source of loving guidance is unconditional. It is to be found inside and outside church and in every nook and corner of life.

It may well be the case we shall need orthodox Christianity yet awhile to keep us on track. Traditionally, in order to remain viable and secure religion has had to surround itself with certainties of belief. Closed theologies provide that safe haven, a refuge and source of fellowship for kindred spirits to promote 'right' living and to offer secure guidance. Historically, religion more than any other institution held the tightest grip upon cultural values until it was prised open by rational thought and rampant materialism. Today one notes subtle shifts of perspectives taking shape even within the most orthodox of church circles as they struggle to stay relevant in modern times. Their preparedness to adapt will ensure their survival. But will they go far enough? And in the right direction? Will they recognise that the day of dogma of certainty is over? Will they give up exclusivity? Will they move with the scientific times? Will they adopt gender equality? Will they acknowledge differences in sexual orientation? Will they purposively preach peace and tolerance of other belief systems? Will they drop outmoded dogma that effectively separates them from other faiths? Will they preach Universal Love? Will they reverse Genesis 1:28?

> Be fruitful and multiply, and replenish the earth and subdue it: and have dominion over the fish of the sea, and over the fowl of the air and over every living thing that moveth upon the earth.

Will they emphasise a respect for and partnership with earth, and preach conservation of its treasures? We detect that some of those questions are being addressed. The process has begun. A tentative and insignificant start maybe, but it has begun, so the answer is surely yes, given time. One senses we have entered a transitory period. Even so, as we look around the world at the consequences of that chilling cry 'If God be for us who can be against us?' the sight is almost unbearable. Changes must come from within individuals, from the workings of our innate spiritual faculty whispering its eternal truth: 'God is for us all'. We are, without doubt, in for a long, hard haul. But triumph we will, ultimately, for in us is the seed of eternal wisdom.

FUNDAMENTAL HUMAN ERRORS

If ever there was an age that needed an anchorage it is this one. To meet this challenge Christianity must leach its many prejudices, particularly those relating to the female half of the human race. The third millennium female will not tolerate religion wholly dominated by masculine symbolism. For two thousand years the idealisation of Mary the Virgin has proven deeply damaging to both men and women, since the connotation of purity placed upon virginity casts a shadow on the glory of natural procreation. The accepted doctrine of the virgin birth and the chosen version of the Adam and Eve story have seriously obscured the rich parallel between sexuality and spirituality. In so doing something precious has been lost, a God-given gift laid to waste. Pagels tells of another version of the Adam and Eve story taken from a Nag Hammadi codex known as the *Hypostasis of the Archons*:

> And the spirit-endowed Woman came to Adam and spoke with him, saying, 'Arise, Adam.' And when he saw her, he said, 'It is you who have given me life; you shall be called "Mother of the living" – for it is she who is my mother. It is she who is the Physician, and the Woman, and She Who Has Given Birth.' …Then the Female Spiritual Principle came in the Snake, the Instructor, and taught them, saying…'You shall not die…Rather, your eyes shall open, and you shall become like gods, recognising evil and good…' [In Gnostic writings the serpent symbolises divine wisdom.]

The negative effect of the Old Testament version of the Adam and Eve story lingers on, its psychology deeply ingrained into our culture. How much gentler understanding there might have been between men and women in Christian cultures had those early scribes chosen a version less sexually discriminating. (We note women do not fare much better in many world religions, their situation appallingly worse in some extreme sects.)

The stories of Christ's healing miracles are of a different order. They offer a choice and will probably continue to do so in the foreseeable future. Those wishing to absorb a literal belief in miracles can happily do so since their message of Love's power of healing filter through the rich symbolism they offer. The doctrine of Mary the Virgin does not fall into this category. Its introduction was an unfortunate one to say the least. In so saying, one is acutely aware of how deeply offensive this view is to those whose faith centres reverently upon traditional concepts of the Blessed Virgin. Yet, though we travel from different perspectives we all arrive with reverence at the mystery of birth. Pasternak sums it up perfectly, ending with a delightful touch of humour. He has Dr Zhivago say:

> It has always seemed to me that every conception is immaculate and that this dogma concerning the Mother of God expresses the idea of motherhood. At the moment of childbirth, every woman has the aura of isolation, as though she were abandoned, alone. Man is as irrelevant to this vital moment as if he had had no part in it and the whole thing had dropped from heaven. It is the woman by herself, who brings

forth her progeny, and herself carries it off to some back-stage of life, a quiet, safe place for a cradle. Alone, in silence and humility, she feeds and rears the child. The Mother of God is asked to 'pray zealously to her Son of God', and the words of the psalm are put into her mouth: 'My soul doth magnify the Lord and my spirit hath rejoiced in God my Saviour. For he hath regarded the low estate of his handmaiden: for behold, from henceforth all generations shall call me blessed' It is because of her child that she says this. He will magnify her (for He that is mighty hath done to me great things'); He is her glory. Any woman could say it. For every one of them, God is in her child. Mothers of great men must have this feeling particularly, but then, at the beginning, all women are mothers of great men – it isn't their fault if life disappoints them later.

Edith Walter also saw the story of the Nativity in spiritual terms: Mary's moment of *cosmic consciousness* (though she would not have used Bucke's terminology) recorded in Luke 1:28–35, was when she received knowledge that she was to become pregnant with no ordinary child. Blessed is she indeed among women. Joseph, with love and understanding, protected her, took her out of harm's way to a secret, lowly place. There the Christ child was born, the natural seed of Joseph; an advanced soul destined to shape the minds of men and women forever with his simple doctrine of Love. He was no freak of nature, not God in the image of man. He was man in the image of God. That is the true miracle. Given that Jesus' physical birth was meant to be of a virgin who had conceived him spiritually, it is reasonable to expect that he would have specifically referred to this event himself. He did not do so because it was not the case. The invention occurred after his death. Nowhere in his teaching did Jesus of Nazareth cast a shadow over sexuality as something to be hidden, intrinsically shameful and sinful. These attitudes are a direct legacy of the doctrine of the Virgin Birth. Christ was not interested in denigrating the body in order to elevate the soul. His teaching was essentially one of compassion for the human condition.

In the New Testament Gospel attributed to Matthew, we read:

> Behold a virgin shall be with child and shall bring forth a son and they shall call his name Emanuel, which being interpreted is 'God in Us'

> (Matthew 1:23)

Matthew was quoting from Isaiah 7:14. The Rev. David Jenkins, Bishop of Durham, points out the shifts that take place when translating from one language to another; in this case from Hebrew into Greek. The Bishop tells us that *parthenos* usually means 'virgin' or 'maiden', but in Hebrew, the original language in which Isaiah's prophecy was written, the word used meant 'young woman'. Had the original translator chosen a word closer to 'young woman', men and women might have been spared considerable pain and confusion.

Logically, Jesus must have been born of natural conception. How could the Son of God be so unfair as to command us to 'Be ye perfect even as I am' when he had such a head start, born perfect whilst we were meant to be born in sin? The perfection referred to is the birth of divine love within the soul of an imperfect human being. A realistic recognition of our human condition depends upon that being the case.

MAN – A FREE SPIRIT

To reiterate, religion is the finite recognition of the infinite. In re-emphasising the distinction between religion and the spiritual we immediately come up against 2,000 years of words used in their historical, emotional and theological connotations, where spirituality, God and religion are seen as mutually inclusive. Traditionally, religion has significantly more to do with theological constructions and man's interpretation of spiritual matters than the pure essence of its founder's message. Where there is a vacuum to be filled in our understanding the temptation is to fill it with wild fantasies. An example of this can be found in at least one website on the Internet of an attempt to surround Dr Maurice Bucke's treatise, the ink hardly dry, with a complicated theological construction. Imagination, like everything else about us as human beings, has advantages as well as distinct disadvantages. When we don't understand we imagine. We invent.

Christian theology, as it evolved during those early centuries AD, profoundly shifted the relationship between man and his spiritual self. Its theology and authoritative hierarchy of the priesthood as guardians of the Holy Sacraments took over man's innate spirituality claiming sole possession, so that religion and spirituality became fused and confused. You were a believer or you were not. You were religious or you were heathen. To be outside a faith was to be outside spirituality. Salvation was achieved exclusively through a belief in the only begotten Son of God. The concept of the Son of God as a supernatural being has induced a split from reality. The truth is no religion has ownership of our spirituality. God and creation are indivisible, not God and religion.

In the Western hemisphere the word 'God' removes us, psychologically, one step away from recognition of our innate spirituality to the extent that many barely recognise its existence outside a religious community. In Christian theology God resides somewhere 'out there'. In centuries past, and indeed in our own, 'He' is a wise old man with a flowing white beard sitting on his throne on a cloud in the sky. For millions this imagery gives great comfort and a deep sense of security. This is our dilemma. To question this loving, simple faith is to encroach upon something meaningful and preciously held. We need to tread carefully whilst recognising that mankind's innate spirituality is evolving and will gain maturity and insight all in good time. When we come to understand that God is not simply out there, somewhere remote from us, but a living power within all things, including us, that God is creation itself, we can comfortably interchange words like God, Divinity, Spirituality and Creation without confusion. We shall come to see more clearly how the power of love, the most potent of creation's energies, is working its purpose out through human awareness of that energy; body and soul have been given a capacity to achieve and to enjoy a seamless relationship with an intelligent universe.

Buddhism and Hinduism (and other ancient Eastern philosophies) kept things a little more simplified. They do not separate God from man, though here too human beings intervened by hijacking the root gnostic vision of the founder member by developing many sects, idolatries and ritual practices. Witness also the Untouchables, though discrimination against castes was made illegal in India in 1947. Spirituality, for the mass of people, became significantly more religious than spiritual, but the concept of a 'Spiritual Birth' is preserved as a direct experience equal to that of the founder member, hence a natural acceptance of Nirvana, Brahmic Splendour and Enlightenment. For Eastern religions God *is* a unifying power, *is* the Absolute, *is* the Wholeness of Being, one and the same.

Today, Western countries are *de facto* secular societies, but not bereft of the milk of human kindness as our nineteenth-century ancestors might have predicted. Innate spirituality is a pretty tough faculty. It thrives and survives challenges from dictatorships, fundamentalist regimes and the morass of commercial materialism found in most secular societies. Innate spiritual qualities are evident wherever humans are in the world. What else are acts of unconditional sacrifice for others, our creativity, compassion, appreciation of art, beauty and form, a passionate concern for planet earth and all its creatures, our profound distress with man's cruelty to man, the thrill of discovery, an unconditional acceptance of 'difference' in our fellow man, our passion for liberty and justice, our sense of awe at the wonder of creation and passionate concern for its ecology? One could continue *ad infinitum* – that powerful energy of Love/God permeates all. What else are we to call these human attributes if not the product of an innate spirituality? Is it so hard to believe that these gifts of love are as much the property of an honest atheist as of the religious? The answer comes down to choice. We are free to choose what we believe to be the source of our humanity, without penalty. Love is unconditional. However, we might be surprised to learn how many *do* recognise an innate spirituality residing within their consciousness as a connective force with 'something', however vaguely defined. Still others, ordinary men and women of today, are privileged to have found that connective force that Jesus a son of man demonstrated with staggering impact.

A Biblical Evaluation?

The Nag Hammadi Gnostic Gospels give new insights into the character of Jesus the man. They reveal his profound grasp of human nature. People privy to an inner circle of esoteric knowledge wrote the Gnostic Gospels. They make for strange reading. Jesus is portrayed as a sophisticated, deep thinker addressing the inner man as a philosopher might. Practically devoid of historical reference and cultural narrative, they appear more as a series of 'jottings', as if the writers were concerned to record the moment or thought before it was lost. In marked contrast, the Jesus of the New Testament addresses people of humble origins in simple parable and symbolism, making his message readily available to everyone. In general, the Gnostic Gospels lack the power of poetic prose, dramatic impact and continuity found in the traditional gospels of Matthew, Mark, Luke and John. Some entries are repetitive, some suffer from gaps in the aged parchments, in some others the language is obscure, esoteric, even enigmatic, while others leap out with striking clarity and truth. Collectively, the Gnostic Gospels appear to supply sufficient material to inform an integrated publication with the gospels of Matthew, Mark, Luke and John; that is to say, of translation and interpretation without compromising the power of the poetic prose of the New Testament version of the four Gospels. Somewhere, at some point, might we look forward to a group of scholars brave enough to take up the challenge? It is an interesting prospect.

★

Will the Nag Hammadi codices ever be enough to bring down the walls of Jericho? Hardly, it will need a little bit of weight from the might of science. But will Joshua care enough to journey to Jericho? Well, his interest *is* aroused. He *has* turned his face to the fight. The mighty giant *has* begun a study of man's consciousness and in so doing has stumbled across something dubbed 'The God Spot', but more of that in Chapter Four. In the following chapter we learn how, according to Dr Bucke, 'The God Spot' began its long evolutionary journey eons ago when it emerged in the mind of man as a tiny spark of divinity.

★

Chapter Three

An Overview

The Mystic

Neither shall they say, lo here!
Or lo there! For behold,
The Kingdom of God is within you.

Luke 17:21

AN EVOLUTIONARY THEORY OF CONSCIOUSNESS

Dr Maurice Bucke was a nineteenth-century psychiatrist
working in Canada. Penguin New York first published
his treatise in 1901. In it he identifies three layers of
consciousness: *simple*, *self* and *cosmic* (which we look at
later in this chapter). These he relates to an
evolutionary theory. His treatise was remarkably bold
for his time, breaking the mould of two thousand years
of Western traditional thinking. He arrived at this
evolutionary perspective following an experience from
which, he said, he learned more in a few seconds than
in months or years of study. He expresses his
experience in the third person:

> He was in a state of quiet, almost passive enjoyment.
> All at once, without warning of any kind he found
> himself wrapped around as it were by a flame colored
> cloud. For an instant he thought of fire, some sudden
> conflagration in the great city, the next he knew that
> the light was himself. Directly afterwards came upon

him a sense of exultation, of immense joyousness accompanied or immediately followed by an intellectual illumination quite impossible to describe. Into his brain streamed one momentary lightening flash of the Brahmic Bliss, leaving thenceforward for always an aftertaste of heaven. Among other things he did not come to believe, he saw and *knew* that the Cosmos is not dead matter but a living Presence, that the soul of man is immortal, that the universe is so built and ordered that without peradventure all things work together for the good of each and all, that the foundation principle of the world is what we call love and that the happiness of every one is in the long run absolutely certain. He claims that he learned more within the few seconds during which the illumination lasted than in previous months or even years of study, and that he learned much that no study could ever have taught.

Bucke goes on to say that those few moments proved 'ineffaceable' and that it was not possible to forget or ever to doubt the truth of what had been presented to his mind. This same experience is essentially identical to personal contemporary accounts found in Survey 2003. It is the *peak* experience among a range of *cosmic conscious* experiences (though Bucke does not specifically make that distinction). He sees *cosmic consciousness* as an innate spiritual faculty that has been evolving over millenniums, incidents of which, he considers, are increasing and gathering momentum within the world's populations. Today, building on Bucke's insight, we see more clearly how *cc* is, in fact, an additional awareness that emerges from an innate spirituality.

It seems likely Darwin was Bucke's launch-pad. Bucke's thinking correlates with a Darwinian principle of natural selection, consciously or subconsciously. We should pause to remind ourselves here that natural selection does not necessarily mean random selection. Is evolution necessarily a blind groping having no goals, pure blind chance? Why should it not be a systematic process within which are self-generated goals? There appears no good reason to assume order does not emerge from chaos. *Cosmic consciousness* tells us we live in a purposeful, intelligent universe. To date, no scientific discovery has proven to be an ultimate truth. Further insights might subject Darwin's work to further refinements. True, humankind's most primitive instinct is one of survival of the fittest. However, we are the only creatures on earth with an evolving capacity to rise above self-interest into higher cognitive functions of communication. This does not have the appearance of the outcome of blind chance. Discoveries highlight our potential and progress our understanding of an evolutionary journey. Bucke appears to be the first person to attach a Darwinian perspective to man's spiritual strivings. In fact, pushing Darwin's theory to include man's spirituality as part of his evolution of consciousness is such a simple idea it required someone to state the obvious. Obvious, that is, to Bucke, but regrettably to this day still not obvious to those whose faith is deeply held and rooted in the theology that has evolved around Christianity. From a purely rational viewpoint the evolution of consciousness into higher forms of consciousness is a

Darwinian idea. Darwin himself shows how the difference between the mind of man and the higher animals is one of degree and not of kind, an idea consistent with Bucke's theory of an evolved consciousness shared first with other creatures and becoming more complex in humankind. In his *Origin of the Species*, Darwin did not appear to view spirituality as innate. However, he conceded:

> The belief in spiritual agencies naturally follows from other mental powers. The moral sense perhaps affords the best and highest distinction between man and the lower animals...

Elsewhere in his *Decent of Man* he expresses this sentiment:

> ...having risen, though not through his own exertions, to the very summit of the organic scale; and the fact of his having thus risen, instead of having been aboriginally placed there, may give him some hope for a still higher destiny in the distant future.

HINDSIGHT

One has to approach Bucke's research findings with the caution of hindsight. Writing at the end of the nineteenth century Bucke would have had little or no reliable research data to support his treatise. What there was would have been crude by modern standards. He appears unconsciously innocent of statistical rigour. Many 'conclusions' are therefore pure speculation: e.g. a survey finding on the incidence of colour blindness made no distinction between disease causation (which might have been high) and congenital colour blindness. The five physical senses – taste, touch, sight, hearing and smell – are grouped together with properties such as imagination, intellect, musicality and so on. It is a reminder of how rapidly we have advanced in accumulated knowledge and how aware we are today of vistas yet unexplored.

Elitism is present in his work, some of which can be understood in the context of an age when hierarchical social structures were viewed as natural and therefore went largely unchallenged. His writings reflect the gender, racial and class prejudices of his day, but regrettably Bucke's work displays a little more than a touch of spiritual pride. He believed a parental pedigree superior in physique, health, intellect and spirituality was an essential pre-requisite of a *cosmic conscious* offspring. Furthermore, the parental couple must be wholly compatible, one with the other. Fortunately, naïve, romanticised views cannot be taken too seriously. Possibly, the clue to this notion lies in Bucke's life experience. He suffered a profound personal trauma in his early childhood. Both his parents died within a few years of each other. The repercussions of this tragedy stayed with him. He left home at age sixteen years to escape from an unhappy home life. Was Bucke affected by a natural idealisation of his lost parents, so dear to his memory? His wish to place them on a pedestal powerfully suggests this to be the case. As human beings, we are, at all times, profoundly influenced by early life experiences. Bucke, as a psychiatrist, would have been aware of this, but it would appear the knowledge had not been applied to his personal circumstances.

Some of the language used by Dr Bucke would not be acceptable in our somewhat over sensitive 'politically correct' society. An illustration of this can be seen in his view of *cosmic conscious* man as a member of a race set apart, almost another species. 'A race set apart' is a phrase that has uncomfortable connotations for post-holocaust generations. Clearly he refers to a collective condition of the human race in eons of time when *cosmic consciousness* will have worked its way through to become the norm and we have a world culture unimaginably different from our own.

Nevertheless, 'a race set apart' suggests superiority and segregation. This is a clear lapse of the *cosmic conscious* perspective. Far from being superior or separate, the *cc* person is a wholly integrated human being, at one with the human condition in compassionate understanding of its frailties and strengths. The life of Edith Walters demonstrated this. She would not have seen herself as one of a race set apart; chosen, yes, but not one of another race. Edith Walters was an imperfect vessel that carried the purity of divine love with natural humility. The impulse of her devout followers was to place her upon a pedestal. She was constantly at pains to bring them into a reality state. She knew that the greater the gift of divine love, the greater the peril of what St John of the Cross condemned as 'The peril of spiritual gluttony'. This truth in itself is proof, if we should ever need it, that *cc* man is, and always will be, an integrated member of the human race. Bucke obviously saw certain logic to his vision of a race set apart. Even if it were true, which manifestly it is not, it was unwise to have said so. Wisdom is greater than truth.

The *cosmic conscious* person of today is merely a continuum of the evolutionary process and does not reflect an emergence of 'a race set apart'. That threat arises from science, from the choices laid at our feet in consequence of scientific activity. Bucke could not have remotely envisaged the advances made in the fields of molecular biology, nanotechnology and the impact of man's intervention in manipulating the human DNA. Bernard Shaw said:

> God created man in His image and man is forever returning the doubtful compliment.

The future perils inherent in genetic engineering outweigh its exciting possibilities. It has already become imperative we maintain a careful watch on our arrogant streak and allow our spiritual intelligence to inform our direction in order to avoid 'returning the doubtful compliment'.

The arrival of aerial navigation fired Bucke's imagination to the point where he allowed himself to be carried away by it. He believed that it would eradicate national boundaries, cities would no longer be needed, language barriers would disappear and all would live in harmony without hardship or toil. Bucke was an incurable romantic. He provides his critics with plenty of ammunition, which they may wish to use in an attempt to discredit his treatise. Certainly it becomes necessary to disentangle his sundry social perceptions from his revolutionary treatise. Failure to do so would be to miss something of great importance. The world moves on and no more swiftly than did the pace of the twentieth century. Bucke's lofty Victorian tone reflects nineteenth-century cultural norms. Fortunately, the merit of Bucke's treatise does not rest on detail but on the depth and breadth of its vision. It is a vision that takes us straight into our twenty-first century scientific age, a watershed work that creates a paradigm shift towards a new age of enlightenment. I believe Bucke was used by God to further our understanding of our spiritual selves. His work is a vital link in our understanding of consciousness.

All this serves to illustrate our essential humanity: that will never leave us. The perception mankind has of saintliness is an illusion; an idealisation of how we think divinity is manifested in human nature. Those who have entered the *peak cosmic conscious* perspective know that that event is a beginning of a journey, not an end. There is no such thing as perfection, in human terms. One hundred years on from Bucke and from when Edith Walters began her spiritual journey, we are entering an age in which we can accept our *cosmic* faculty with maturity, easily and naturally. We understand that the *cosmic* capacity, that perfect spark of divinity, is an integral part of who we are, having respect for individual temperament and personality. Divine love works its miracle in complete harmony with the wondrous diversity of human nature. We can safely assign notions of sainthood to the history books.

BUCKE'S EVOLUTIONARY CHART

Interestingly, Bucke draws a comparative chart between the age at which the average development of a given faculty appears in the individual and its historical emergence in the human race. For example; today, there appear to be many more babies who respond to the sound of music than there are adults who are tone deaf. If this impression were to be supported by clear evidence, Bucke would say man's musicality is firmly established (it cannot now be lost) because of the high incidence of musically receptive babies in the population, but if congenital tone deafness in adults were significantly high, musicality, though firmly established, would register on the evolutionary scale as a relatively new faculty.

The contrast between the five tonal chants of early ancestors and Schoenberg's 'Pierrot Lunaire' twelve-note composition suggests a protracted evolutionary journey followed by recent rapid acceleration. But one wonders, at what stage did complexity arrive? Herbert Girardet tells us: 'The intricate, polyphonic songs of the pygmies in today's rain forests are amongst the most beautiful music ever created.' Globally our musical sense appears well developed. It would seem that most people can sing along with a tune, though not everyone has the capacity to be musically literate and only a few possess exceptional musical talent. Greater exposure to stimuli, however, promotes fulfilment of individual potential. Environment and evolution are intimately entwined.

Bucke speculates that full colour vision too is a recent arrival. He reminds us that Democritus spoke of four colours: black, red, yellow and white. Aristotle referred to a tri-colour rainbow. Poets of the *Odyssey*, *Iliad* and the Bible decline to mention a colour for the most vivid blue seas on the planet. This tells us something about individual poets but nothing about gifted painters and cloth-weavers of the time. Indeed, we can speculate that it merely indicates a paucity of words to describe shadings. How can we know? Granted it raises interesting speculations if not strong inferences. Today a congenital colour deficiency is still with us. According to Bucke's theory, studies to measure the emergence of colour definition capacity in infant populations and comparing its ratio with colour deficiency in adults would indicate the evolutionary timescale of full colour vision.

Bucke sees dreams as another indicator of personal maturity and how sophisticated we are on the collective evolutionary timescale. It becomes important to know the ratio within populations of people who dream in black and white, in colour, hear music, poetry and experience dance in their dreams. For the few, dreams are a springboard to creativity in the arts and in scientific endeavour. Some very creative people extract life skills, self-awareness and a sense of direction from dream interpretation. Lucid dreams, a kind of wakeful dream when *you* consciously will the dream to continue or, if unpleasant, you decide to exit the dream, are also particularly interesting. In lucid dreams colours are more vivid, everything more real and vibrant. They often promote creativity and enhance self-confidence. People's dream patterns are important clues to levels of emotional and spiritual development in the individual. Bucke sees that: 'In any race the stability of any faculty is in proportion to the age of the faculty in the race.'

Bucke must have outraged his contemporaries by declaring spirituality as simply another faculty alongside all the others. He is a bit like the little boy in Hans Andersen's fairy tale, who seeing things the way they are calls out from the crowd, 'The Emperor, the Emporer! He has no clothes!'

Bucke sees our spirituality developing to a sophisticated extent, becoming all pervasive, more deeply grounded into our psychological development, less dependent upon the prop of religion. He considers it cannot now be lost. Judged by Bucke's own criterion, however, it is a relatively young arrival on the evolutionary ladder. He sought to explore the advent of *cosmic consciousness*. He saw clearly that at some point our individual innate spirituality could evolve into conscious awareness of its *cosmic* dimension. His 1901 survey shows that when it does occur, (the *peak* of) *cosmic consciousness* is experienced on average between ages thirty and forty years. Survey 2003 indicates a wider age range. As it advances in strength through the centuries, the age it manifests in individuals will get younger.

Excitingly, Chapter Five provides examples of the *pcc* events experienced by a seven-year old child and a fourteen-year-old, which strongly suggests there have to be many more *pcc* youngsters out there. One wonders how they might assimilate such a powerful event on their own. Some may accept it easily and naturally. In whatever way it is handled initially, it could not be forgotten, perhaps imbedded in the unconscious, their psyche governed by it. We have much to learn. That children do have spiritual experiences is reasonably well documented. However, we specifically refer to the *peak* of *cosmic consciousness*.

Obviously, special research measures and techniques would be required for infants/juveniles. The occurrence of *peak cosmic consciousness* in the very young would explain why some rare individuals in adulthood are outstandingly mature – and recognisably so to others – but within themselves quite happily unaware of having received a special guiding insight. On Bucke's terms, they would be far ahead of their time. Bucke expects not only a consistently progressive age reduction to work its way down through successive centuries, but also numbers of *cosmic conscious* people increasing with each passing century as it does so.

We are all well aware of how spirituality can be obscured by indifference and our negligence. The same can be said of any other faculty lying dormant, its potential unrealised or unrecognised, (sensory faculties aside). Our spirituality may become muddied, confused and caught up in a variety of psychic phenomena, sometimes the product of hysteria, or heightened imaginings born out of delusions of grandeur or worse; just plain incoherent pseudo religiosity. Historically, Bucke sees this as symptomatic of an evolving innate primitive striving that with the passage of time – possibly measured in millenniums – will find its culmination in a clearly understood cosmic perspective. When that day arrives humankind will have come of age; we will have reached maturity. *Cosmic consciousness* will have become the norm and be accepted naturally. The prospect offers a bright beacon of hope for our future on this planet.

BUCKE'S SPIRITUAL EVOLUTION OF MANKIND

SIMPLE CONSCIOUSNESS
(Early Man)

———————————————————

Barbaric. Little awareness of self.
No moral sensibilities.

(The simple consciousness mentality, still present within today's society)

SELF-CONSCIOUSNESS
(Birth of Modern Man. Language/value systems)

———————————————————

Growing awareness of self and empathy for others.
Spiritual search for meaning. Birth of belief systems.
Continuously developing moralities.

COSMIC CONSCIOUSNESS
(Arrived, possibly, three millennia ago)

———————————————————

Knowledge of immortality.
The attributive source of love in mankind
understood, absolutely.
Spiritually connected in creation.
Religious theories redundant.
Sacred values held sacrosanct.
Cosmic consciousness, imbedded in humanity;
an evolutionary process still in its infancy.

Sufi Teaching
God sleeps in the rocks
Dreams in the plants
Stirs in the animals
And awakens in Man

Simple Consciousness

Around two and half million years ago Palaeolithic man would have been barely distinguishable from other creatures on earth since he would be almost wholly in the *simple conscious* state. Bucke views *simple consciousness* as the first rung of the ladder. *Simple consciousness* is to be found in the whole of the animal kingdom, modern homo sapiens included. Obviously, many creatures of the wild possess attributes that surpass man's abilities: stunning innate navigational skills; acute vision; highly developed sense of smell and hearing; incredible powers to predict climatic and seasonal changes; and numerous other instinctive behaviours, many of which are beyond our understanding as yet. Therefore, the *simple conscious* things man shares with his fellow creatures includes only the basics; that is to say we are aware of our bodies, our limbs, our mate, offspring, our pack, herd, clan etc. and our immediate territory and food supply. Above all man shares consciousness with all other creatures. Bucke's correlation does not include primitive life forms – insects, micro-organisms etc. Were he alive today he might have considered it necessary to do so.

Self-Consciousness

Bucke suggests that over eons of time man emerged out of mere simple consciousness into *self-consciousness*. Palaeolithic man is as far removed from modern man as he is from the highest primates in the non-human animal kingdom. Palaeolithic man would have had little or no sense of good or evil, and therefore little concept of shame. As he entered the *self-conscious* state his eyes were opened; his innocence lost. He became responsible for his own conduct. A sense of awareness was born and with it, faced with his fallibility, a sense of guilt and remorse; the metaphoric Garden of Eden.

The emergent *self-conscious* man now recognises himself as a distinct entity. Gradually he develops powers of abstraction, objectivity, intelligence, reason, reflection, judgement, imagination, compassion, love and much more. He becomes increasingly spiritually aware. Crucially, he develops advanced linguistic skill. From intelligence and language spring an evolving sense of morality, shifting and changing from culture to culture and from age to age. Bucke sees that in *self-conscious* man his moral sense is the most vulnerable to collapse. Time and time again we see moral regression at times of acute social disorder – anarchy, war, famine, poverty – as well as in climates of competitive greed and unbridled materialism. As man's moral fibre grows stronger from generation to generation, its cyclical lapses will become less frequent. This is where spiritually mature people come in to add their weight to the positive forces at work in an increasingly intricate and complex world.

COSMIC CONSCIOUSNESS

It should be noted here that the specific experience to which Bucke refers is in fact the peak experience from a whole range of cosmic consciousness intensities. Bucke referred to it as the 'Full Brahmic Splendour'.

In Hinduism, deathlessness is the soul. The soul has the potential to rise from this body to the highest reaches of the Light (*peak cosmic consciousness*); i.e.

immortality. The mortal body is Death. The Soul is Life. Hinduism is not only founded upon the experience of divine light but takes it as its ultimate goal. The Nyaya and Vaishesika, two of the many schools of thought within Hinduism, embrace the concept of life as forms of atoms extending to the cosmos, the entire universe. Such insight is a stunningly advanced intellectual concept, a classic example of esoteric knowledge gained from the *peak cosmic consciousness*. Around three thousand years later, scientists have encountered this truth via the discipline of quantum physics. Hinduism recognises a divine reality that permeates the everyday world of the senses. This they see as the relationship between God (Brahman) and the soul (Atman). The source of its inspiration lies in the specific experience of light and ecstasy known as Brahmic Splendour (*peak cosmic consciousness*). In the Upanishads (800–500 BC) we find a conversation between Prajapati and the God Indura, which tells of this mortal body appropriated by Death but which is the standing ground of Deathlessness – the Soul. The Upanishads are said to be the oldest surviving record of mysticism, and yet still they correspond to today's accounts.

We are assuredly spiritual beings by nature, and although many have the potential to reach the *peak* of *cosmic consciousness*, thus far in our evolutionary development it would seem relatively few have attained it. However, this may be a superficial impression since few people talk about their most sacred moments for a variety of reasons, one being that words are found to be inadequate. Bucke sees that this capacity to reach a cosmic sense is a gift of love proportionally found in each individual. He suggests our whole spiritual evolutionary progression on this planet is three-dimensional: 1) parental selection (gene transmission); 2) influences of the physical and cultural environment each life happens to inhabit and; 3) the individual's psychological environment. This last condition is crucial. The *cosmic consciousness* cannot enter an unreceptive frame of mind, neither can its natural expression be induced or achieved by study any more than we can mould our children into something beyond their natural capacities. So, we are back to genetics. What we are born with is what we have the potential to become and each responsible for realising our own potential.

The ratio of nurture/nature eludes us still. On the one hand we see how outstanding innate talent can rise like a phoenix out of whatever pit of environmental ashes it happens to be found in. On the other we observe how wasteful nature is of humanity's gifts and talents, how careless, how random, how dependent upon luck, on being in the right place at the right time, upon having the 'right' kind of parents or mentors with the right kind of awareness and imagination, and sometimes, importantly, parents with the right kind of bank balance. Fortunately, native intelligence and spiritual insight are gifts hardly dependent upon time and place and certainly not upon material wealth.

Crucially, the internal environment must be right. In this context the whole person is the environment; his/her level of self-awareness, compassion, spontaneity, generosity of spirit, developed intuitiveness and willingness to understand the reality of the living soul enjoined with a profound yearning to connect. This is the soil in which the soul flourishes. Just as there are grades of excellence within all human talents so there are degrees of spiritual maturity among those possessing *peak cosmic consciousness* and those who do not, but without that profound yearning to connect with one's soul, the door remains closed. *Blessed are they that mourn for they shall be comforted.* A parallel may be drawn with people who may go through their entire lives with hidden talents unexpressed such as art, poetry or music, never having found the conditions or the trigger to make the discovery, yet they may possess more talent than many who did.

SPIRITUAL PRIDE

The Bible tells us many are called but few are chosen. 'Chosen' is a word to be used sparingly and with extreme caution. To be chosen is to be elevated above others. It suggests that to be chosen is to be chosen for a purpose. It is a word best confined to that definition. Nelson Mandela, Martin Luther King, Mahatma Ghandi appear not to have received the *peak* moment of *cosmic consciousness,* but no one could doubt they were men of destiny chosen to fulfil a mission. Driven by a deep undercurrent of spirituality, maturity of character and intellect, the force of their calling left them little choice.

The giants we all know about. They conditioned the whole course of history: Jesus Christ, Zoroasthra, Gautama Buddha, Mohammed and others. We walked in their footsteps imposing our own bloody, turbulent history. Upon their word civilisations were shaped and destroyed or largely distorted by mankind's highly complex drives and passions. Yet miraculously the imprint of divine love they taught lives on. In their wake sprang inspiration for great works of art, music, literature and deeds of love and sacrifice among notables and ordinary folk alike, but for the average person possession of that wondrous gift is a private matter. It would appear most are free to live their lives quietly, choosing to remain silent. They know all things are working together for the ultimate good of the human race, albeit exceedingly slowly, but inexorably. They know *peak cosmic consciousness* is both natural and miraculous, like creation itself. It is, then, a natural phenomenon occurring among ordinary people who in every respect are indistinguishable from anyone else. As we have noted, our human perception of what advanced spirituality is, or should be, does not necessarily lead to the possession of *peak cosmic consciousness* experience. A Harlem nightclub singer is as good a candidate as a high church dignitary. In Bucke's scheme of things spirituality is not a sideshow. We may deny its expression but not its existence. It cannot be denied anymore than can the existence of intelligence, imagination and intuition. Within this context, embellishing *peak cosmic consciousness* with grandeur and saintly aura and surrounding it with a complex theological creed or cult is inappropriate and entirely unnecessary, and in this third millennium, entirely unproductive.

We have outlived a belief in Father Christmas, like a small child who has 'twigged it' but does not want to let on out of fear she may lose the benefits. The altruistic child will feel that by bursting the bubble he will be letting his parents down. Anyway, it's magic, it's fun! So why let go?

It is time we grew up. It is time we understood that possession of divine love does not transform us into demi-gods, nor do we become saints lifted into a sphere of excellence, set apart from others. The gift of love is to be shared not closeted. This is the message by example from Edith Walters and other advanced souls. Human beings are the channels for the universal flow of spirituality, not its source. Bucke's treatise (but not his elitist views) plants our feet firmly on solid ground. There is nothing abnormal about *peak cosmic consciousness*. It is not, as Western theologies proclaim, something conferred upon us by a remote deity lifting man out and away from his/her common humanity. In addition, Bucke particularly specifies our spirituality as an innate faculty not to be confused with religiosity. Religion is something grafted on by choice, a by-product of our overwhelming need to find meaning and assurance. As such it has potential power to touch the deepest source of our spirituality when not bound up in autocracy and power politics.

So, here is a conundrum. Not supernatural or supranormal but a spark of divinity residing within the human psyche, a flash point connecting our souls with the universe. And we are expected to regard this as normal? Yes, we must. If the *peak cosmic consciousness* is to become increasingly prevalent then we had better take it in our stride and greet it with maturity and humility. What is higher consciousness if it is not an evolutionary force actualising a possibility in the universe that has created it?

CONCLUSION

In his book, Bucke appears to underestimate the human drive to come together in mutual celebration and Holy Communion. He predicts the evolutionary theory will supplant institutionalised religion. Certainly the form will – indeed, must – change. No doubt, given our impressive powers of adaptability we shall find new and deeper expressions of our share of divinity found in creation. Sharing and acknowledging the source of love, of God in us, takes on a role of uttermost significance and beauty. If Bucke's theory is right, we will slowly move into an era in which spirituality will be pursued without the aid of complex theologies and punitive threats of eternal damnation. In fairness to Bucke the nub of his assertion is that mature spirituality renders manmade theological clutter redundant. However, man is a communal being. We draw strength and joy from experiences shared. The more mature the spirituality the more there is to celebrate.

Yes, man *is* on his own, face to face with the reality of his soul, not a remote God above us in the sky somewhere, not God exclusively through mediation of saint or priest, or of a perfect being of a literal virgin birth ossified in fable, but God in us. A Living Birth. The Living Christ. The Living Mohammed. The Living Siddharta Guatama. The original, unadulterated message of those advanced souls was clear: resident in human beings is a source of latent divinity, the ground of all being. This is the very reason why we shall be propelled together in mutual celebration and Holy

Communion without the dubious aid of exclusive theologies.

Those among us who have received *peak cosmic consciousness* know that this is how we will come to terms with our spiritual selves. Most of us are ordinary people with no pretensions to teach the rest how to live since we must grapple with the foibles of our own diverse natures. For most people, in the prevailing climate of today, exposing one's encounter with divinity would be counterproductive. We are all familiar with pseudo, parrot-like incantations of having been 'born again' or 'seen the light' inevitably becoming exposed to ridicule or light-hearted fun. One has to be a strong character to 'come out' and preserve credibility. Bucke makes the point:

> As there are varying shades of 'moral' man within the plane of self consciousness, so people with *cosmic consciousness* would vary in intellectual ability, greater or lesser moral elevation and quality of character.

If it is thought Bucke's vision creates an impression of a dull, bland world, then think again. Given that we will choose to exercise wisdom and restraint in the field of molecular biology, man will be as creation made him: controversial, constructively contentious, inquisitive, diverse, creative, inventive, piercingly astute, fun loving, unique in disposition and character and happily human. Creatures perfect in all thought and action, whatever that means, is an unthinkable prospect. Such a vision is in itself an imperfection. A feeling of having nothing in common with others, of somehow being special has no part in the *cosmic consciousness*. We know where our arrogant pursuit of perfection has led us. *Peak cosmic conscious* man has no room for po-faced piety, straight-laced puritism and sanctimonious hand wringing. In time such imagery will be relegated to our primitive past.

> *Many dangers, toils and snares*
> *I have already come*
> *T'is Grace hath brought me safe so far*
> *And Grace will lead me home*
> *When we been here ten thousand years*
> *Bright shining as the sun*
> *We've no less days to sing God's praise*
> *Than when we first began.*

Amazing Grace

★

A hundred years on from when Bucke faced up to man's spirituality as a natural part of the human consciousness profile, science is poised on the brink of neurological discoveries, drawing nearer to something that has the appearance of a 'God Spot'. The working of the human mind, hitherto explored by philosophy, psychology and psychiatry, has become the subject of new disciplines: neurobiology, genetics, biochemistry, molecular biology, nanobiology among others have opened up new vistas of knowledge.

Many view quantum physics as the most exciting of all sciences. It promises much but it is, relatively, still in its infancy. Particle physics, right from its onset at the turn of the twentieth century, profoundly challenged man's powers of objectivity and continues to do so in the twenty-first. Quantum physics is edging science, very reluctantly, into holistic perspectives. The trick, it would seem, is to balance rational, factual processes with creativity, intuition and working hypotheses. Our power of reason should help. The microscopic study of atomic particles is begging us to look again at the way we see ourselves in the universe. Are we humans separate beings set apart from the rest of creation with the world at our feet for our inspection and exploitation? Or is our consciousness an integral part of that world bonded holistically with creation itself? Many already know the answer to those questions. It would seem that twenty-first-century science is on course to provide its own definitive answer.

★

Chapter Four

An Overview

The Philosopher

Quantum theory points out that the same particles that formed the building blocks of our universe underlie the emergence of consciousness. We are therefore, 'The stuff that stars are made of' and potential heirs to a cosmic consciousness – a feeling of oneness with the universe and each other.

Professor Jean Walters

QUANTUM CONSCIOUSNESS

Disclaimer: Since this book is written by a layman for the layman, the author relies upon the common usage of such words as brain, mind and consciousness and is, therefore, detached from differing definitions placed upon these words by individual neuroscientists and philosophers.

Nearly a century has passed since quantum physics burst upon a brilliant group of European physicists. They were the first to discover the notion of consciousness implicated in the study of particles within the nucleus of the atom under laboratory conditions. They dared not believe it. Albert Einstein and his contemporaries enjoyed a high degree of cooperation and honest debate. They shared their theories and outcomes of experimentations, but all were dancing on a pinhead unable to escape the classical, conventional mould of scientific methodology. They found themselves on the cusp of change faced with a baffling new kind of physics, the physics of miniscule entities, delinquent, perverse, unmanageable and worse, immeasurable. The degree of mental turmoil and emotional frustration endured by these gifted young men was exacerbated by their close proximity to the genius of Einstein and the exacting mind of Niels Bohr, a founding father of quantum physics. Though Einstein's *Theory of Relativity* is in the classical mode and as such is incompatible with quantum physics at critical levels, many assert, as did Bohr in 1920, that Einstein's theory was a springboard for the arrival of quantum physics.[1] Eighty years on and many physicists still struggle with an intractable problem: that awkward theoretical gap between classical physics (macro) and quantum physics (micro). The arrival of quantum physics was a gestalt shift from the classical that says, in effect, that the part is more fundamental than the whole. In quantum physics the whole is more

---

[1] Quantum physics can be traced back to 1859 with Gustov Kichoff's work on radiation. In 1897 JJ Thomson discovered the electron. Planck discovered universal quantum action in 1900. In 1911 Rutherford discovered the atomic nucleus. During the first third of the twentieth century Einstein and his contemporaries Planck, Bohr, Bose, Dirac, Born, Heisenburg, Schrodinger, Erenfest, *et. al.*, advanced our knowledge of particle physics, heralding in the age of quantum mechanics. In 1932, Von Neumann discovered the neutron and placed quantum theory on a firm theoretical basis. For the latter two thirds of the twentieth century quantum physics remained an unsolved mystery, and continues to remain so at the beginning of the twenty-first. This is probably the reason why it has failed to impact upon the general public.

fundamental than the part. It can be seen that the latter subsumes the former. How, now, can there be classical reality of independent parts?

In addition nothing has yet entered the *theory* of quantum physics to accommodate consciousness processes. The fact that human consciousness interacts with the particle in the atom strongly implies a *cosmic* capacity within the brain's neural workings, an idea that has the power to disturb the Western mind nourished by Cartesian[2] influences. As we have seen, *cosmic consciousness* reminds us of the presence of an all-pervasive spiritual faculty within our consciousness, a faculty more potent than any other since it is where our cognitive link with creation is located. Consciousness itself was predominantly the subjective study of philosophy, psychiatry and psychology until recently when it became the subject of exploration in laboratory conditions. A few particle physicists, mathematicians and neurologists have begun the search for quantum coherence in human brain functioning. Consciousness has entered the scientific arena.

Nevertheless, we should remind ourselves that for

---

[2] Rene Descartes (1596–1650). Cartesian philosophy: totally opposite to an Eastern conception of life which sees mind, body and soul i.e. consciousness, matter and spirit, as part of an intelligent universe; the Wholeness of Being. Descartes saw mind and body as separate. This notion infused Western culture and shaped its collective cast of mind. Descartes' philosophy can be viewed as a natural extension of Christian theology and its doctrine of God 'out there' and man born in sin i.e. the separation of body and soul.

the scientific discipline quantum coherence does not necessarily embrace a metaphysical dimension, though there are clear signs of at least a sideways glance in that direction. The obvious question to ask here is, what intriguing feature does *peak cosmic consciousness* have that should arrest the attention of particle physicists? Persistent and unequivocal accounts of a human capacity to enter a timeless dimension should be enough, especially so, since the *peak cosmic conscious* event is the easiest and the most uncomplicated to identify out of the whole range of the bizarre, the strange and, thus far, the inexplicable psychological projections to which human beings are subject. This is because in essence there is little variability within both the actual event and its outcomes among all those privileged to absorb it. They know what particle physicists have now discovered: what was hitherto thought to be 'a lifeless void' is alive with pulsating, dynamic 'intelligence', oscillating energy permeating the cosmos and planet earth. They emerge from that mind-expanding event with the certain knowledge that we are all made of the same stuff as the stars. They understand completely that all things are indivisible and because they are also rational beings they emerge with the realisation that the connecting point with the Wholeness of Being lays within consciousness. The experiencer is left with no choice but to identify this with their living soul.

Such certainty does not properly lie within the domain of scientific enquiry, and since we do not have a mature concept of our spirituality the scientific establishment is not in a position to use metaphysical terminology. One understands the difficulty science has in referring to the soul as a serious entity of the human psyche, since it is often associated with minority cranky idealism and the tragic outcomes of fanatical cults. But that institutional resistance, faced with new and challenging perspectives, is beginning to dissolve.

A MEETING OF MINDS

Some of the world's leading universities are now looking seriously at the input consciousness has upon experimentation and its implications. For example, in 2000 at Tucson, Arizona, a convention was held entitled *Towards a Science of Consciousness*. 'Towards' is an interesting word here, implying that science is ready to face head-on the role of consciousness in the field of particle physics. There is a pioneering spirit to the agenda set by the University of Arizona in its exploration of consciousness. In addition to the usual subjects one would expect – namely neurology, psychology, the biological sciences, class, gender, ethnic consciousness and drug substances – one finds hitherto excluded dimensions such as philosophy, Shamanism, Taoism, Yogic practices, the Tibetan Tantric View and spiritual intelligence, i.e. 'God consciousness', and, of course, particle physics. All this is quite extraordinary. It leads one to hope that consciousness will one day enter the theory of quantum physics.

The inclusion of a metaphysical dimension into the orbit of consciousness studies is a tacit admission that since philosophy and religion emanate from consciousness processes, by extension the concept of 'soul' cannot be ignored. It is the first intimation of a holistic perspective seeping into the study of consciousness. Science has begun to tread new territory foreign to its disciplines and to a highly significant extent foreign to its established tradition. It represents a huge challenge. A study of human consciousness is surely the most difficult of all scientific frontiers, possibly the last frontier when consciousness itself becomes recognised as the ultimate key to further understanding. But how can consciousness study consciousness? Doubtless we shall surmount the insurmountable; such is our faith in the genius of our species. That genius exists at all is indicative of an evolving capacity to be at one with an understanding of space and time. Pierre Chardin observes: 'The consciousness of each of us is evolution looking at itself and reflecting.' The very fact that human beings can link in with an understanding of creation is of enormous significance. Physicist Professor Paul Davies puts it this way:

> We, who are children of the universe – animated star dust – can nevertheless reflect on the nature of that same universe, even to the extent of glimpsing the rules on which it runs. How we have become linked into this cosmic dimension is a great mystery. Yet the linkage cannot be denied. What is man that we might be part of such privilege... through conscious being the universe has generated self-awareness. This can be no trivial detail, no minor by-product of mindless, purposeless forces. We are truly meant to be here.

THE GOD SPOT

Sometime in the future our spirituality may turn out to be found in quantum coherence as an integrative product spanning the entire brain. However, if the functioning of the 'little grey cells' is to be explained in terms of a quantum process, science has first to negotiate its first stumbling block. Quantum coherence needs low temperatures, a few degrees above absolute zero, which should rule out its presence in the warm-blooded human species. We have also to bear in mind that the structures of atoms with which physicists are familiar is fundamentally different from those found in molecular biology.

Professor Stuart Hameroff and colleagues at the University of Arizona have taken a close look at the intricacies of the brain. Inside the brain is a mass of neurons, synapses, dendrites, cytoskeletons and microtubules. Research has revealed interesting possibilities. Interest is centred upon the hollow microtubules. They are so tiny it is difficult to imagine their size since their diameter is measured in nanometres (one thousand millionth of a metre). Microtubules appear to have some role in strengthening the billions of synapses. In general, the function of synapses is to enable firing between neurons. A possibility exists that microtubules themselves may contain insulation properties necessary to sustain a quantum state. Without insulation there can be no quantum coherence. The idea is that quantum coherence must leap the synaptic barrier between neuron and neuron. British mathematician,

Sir Roger Penrose, summing up research in this area, says:

> Our picture then, is some kind of global quantum state which coherently couples the activities taking place within tubes, concerning microtubules collectively right across large areas of the brain... There is no doubt in my own mind that there are significant surprises in store for us.

During the 1980s, Prof. Hameroff of the University of Arizona published several papers on nanotechnology and consciousness. Influenced by Penrose's *The Emperor's New Mind*, the two men developed a model for consciousness using Penrose's 'objective reductionism' which has to do with quantum gravity linked to space-time geometry (understood by the privileged few!).

We ask the question, is *cosmic consciousness* located in quantum consciousness? And if so, since *cosmic consciousness* is a deeper expression of an innate spirituality, might this be keyed into quantum coherence as part of an integrated whole? Should this be the case, *peak cosmic consciousness* would assuredly be its peak manifestation. Were Bucke alive today, he might also have aligned quantum coherence with innate spirituality in his thesis. One hundred years on Dana Zohar, in her *Spiritual Intelligence The Ultimate Intelligence*, identifies this faculty as our spiritual quotient, SQ. She considers our SQ is as open to measurement as EQ, our emotional quotient, and IQ, our intelligence quotient. Zohar points out the need for research into our spiritual nature. It is a daunting prospect but surely not an impossible one. So complex is human nature it has proven difficult to find suitable measurements to accommodate the different kinds of intelligences much less intangibles such as imagination, emotion, and spirituality. Indeed the real question might be whether it is remotely possible to view any one faculty in isolation, since we are by nature integrative, holistic beings. A holistic approach adopted by the behavioural sciences would include spirituality and a clearer understanding of its widespread area of influence in our lives. For example, religion is merely one of a myriad ways of expressing our spiritual selves, but this is a distinction rarely important enough to be noted and so the institutional polarisation between science and spirituality remain relatively intact. Consequently, the waters are decidedly muddied.

One of the first discoveries one makes, when researching neurological studies into consciousness, is the scarcity of work done on the brain *vis-à-vis* religious/spiritual behaviour. Neurology can tell us what neural arrangements within the brain are for sight, hearing, sexual instinct, memory, language skills, emotion, motor skills, musicality and so on, but a location in the brain that led us to dance around the totem poll is almost a taboo idea. More prevalent is a distinct hands-off 'God matters' attitude unless it is viewed as a symptom of a dysfunctional brain. By inference, science stands outside human experience, value free; science and spirituality mutually exclusive.

To a significant degree research into neural functioning in the brain carried out by VS Ramachandran, neurologist, with his colleagues in

California in 1997 and the work of Dr Michael Persinger, neuropsychologist, in Canada has caught a glimpse of the soul's presence within the temporal lobe cortical area. Their research findings were quickly dubbed 'The God Spot' and just as quickly qualified by Ramachandran and Persinger with a distinction carefully made between a response to god topics and the existence of God.

Ramachandran's work with epileptic patients in San Diego has shown a high activity to 'God matters' in the temporal lobe area. During seizure, it appears widespread electrical activity selectively strengthens connections between the temporal lobe area, which gives rise to 'religious' experiences. Linked to a background of extensive knowledge of temporal lobe epilepsy (TLE) Ramachandran was able to make important observations on patients in experimental situation, using electrodes to measure galvanic skin response. Subjects were shown pictures of friends and family members, ordinary everyday objects, unfamiliar faces, religious icons, sexually arousing pictures, extreme acts of violence involving sex and scenes of horror. Some subjects responded to the religious stimulus but displayed a deadened response to other stimuli. A disinterest in normal sexual activity and indifference to man's inhumanity to man reveal a low spiritual capacity.

Ramachandran notes how some TLE patients who were obsessional about religion were also, among other character traits, pedantic, egocentric, lacking in humility, argumentative and arrogant, all of which would rate low on a spiritual quotient scale. In accepting this hypothesis, would it be correct to speculate that one would be left with patients who during epileptic seizures suffer aggravated stimulation of the temporal lobe area whilst in other epileptic subjects it would be counterbalanced with a developed spiritual quotient? A significant degree of SQ is necessary for a genuine and meaningful expression of religious belief. These criteria might also apply in drug-induced states. We note how the psychedelic drugs such as LSD, psilocybin and mescaline can have short-term pleasant effects on some subjects and unpleasant, even terrifying, effects upon others. In meditational practices the innate SQ of participants may partly, if not wholly, condition success/failure rates.

Persinger carried out another important work. His subjects were all psychologically well people. Persinger's work is possibly one of the first of its kind to avoid mental ill health. Volunteers wore helmets that produce micro seizures in the temporal lobe of the brain. A Transcranial Magnetic Simulator emitted powerful magnetic fields onto targeted areas of brain tissue. By applying stimuli to different parts of the brain, Persinger showed that the subcortical temporal lobe contributes to paranormal experiences and beliefs, whilst the temporal lobe cortical area produces more comforting effects such as dream-like states, visions, and a sense of presence often of mystical or religious content. These he identifies as temporal lobe transient events, TLT. This is viewed as the brain's survival kit for times of extreme crisis, which has allowed humans to cope with untold horror, famine, pestilence and so on, thus safely rationalising the 'God Spot'. Persinger tried this experiment on himself. To his amazement he found he experienced 'God'.

Could work with subjects claiming to have recently received *peak cosmic consciousness* advance research? Since its afterglow would still consume recipients, such research could not be entered upon lightly. By definition the original magnificence of a divine encounter cannot be reproduced by artificial means. Even so, given the supreme power of the original *peak cosmic consciousness* any artificial stimuli too soon after the event might carry risks. We do not know the limitation of the human mind to withstand over exposure. Ethics are a serious consideration in all neurological research, and nowhere more so than in 'God matters'. Therefore, given the professional approach we have come to expect in scientific research, there is no good reason why this avenue should not be pursued until a suitable lapse of time after the event.

There will be those who will be deeply shocked and disturbed by the very idea of science meddling with the sacred. I plead with them: please do not fear. Nothing can disprove the presence of divinity. We are the only creatures on earth with the means to explore and to understand the universe and ourselves. This is the gift of divinity itself. 'What should the solving of nature's secrets be? The discovery of God both within and without.' (Goethe.) The question is not whether we should discover knowledge but how we use it when it is found.

Once we completely accept that, consciously or unconsciously, human beings have a spiritual faculty independent of complicity with the idea of a divine energy (usually referred to as God) and independent of a chosen belief system but may also embrace a belief system, we are half way to clearing away our traditional baggage. Then, with definition and assessment procedures in place, experimental outcomes might become less amazing. Ramachandran sums up:

> …whether or not one believes in religious conformity 'genes', it's clear that certain parts of the temporal lobe play a more direct role in the genesis of such experiences than any other part of the brain. And if the personal experiences of Dr Persinger are anything to go by, then this must be true not just of epileptic people but also of you and me.

In the work of Persinger, Ramachandran and others we see that a foundational start has been pioneered. It reveals some very important indications for future exploration into brain functioning.

> My goal as a scientist is to discover how and why religious sentiments originate in the brain, but this has no bearing one way or another on whether God exists or not.

> (Dr Ramachandran)

Persinger has expressed a similar disclaimer. We would agree that this is how it should be. However, the louder scientists proclaim detachment from human values and experience, the more suspect they appear: 'the Lady doth protest too much methinks' (Shakespeare, *Hamlet*).

Another neuroscientist, Gerald Edelman, spells out the enormous potential of the human brain. In that part of the human brain called the cerebral cortex, the higher brain function responsible for thought, language, speech, music, and so on, there are about ten billion neurons. He tells us each of those nerve cells receives connections from the synapses cell sites, of which there are about one million billion in the cortex. (Remember, microtubules are thought to strengthen synapse in their firing between neurons. (Penrose/ Hameroff.) We take a deep breath before Edelman further dazzles us with the fact that: '...if we were to count them, one synapses per second, we would finish counting about 32 million years after we had began.' And if that were not enough to set our minds reeling, he attempts to assist us further:

> Another way of getting the feeling for the numbers of connections in this extraordinary structure is to consider that a large match head's worth of your brain contains about a billion connections... if we consider how connections might be variously combined, the number would be hyper astronomical – in the order of ten followed by millions of zeros.

We need to pinch ourselves: Edelman is talking about *one* human brain. Staggeringly, there are 'only' (sic) about ten followed by eighty zeros worth of positively-charged particles in the whole universe. Still Edelman does not let us off the hook as we struggle to absorb a further fact: 'The densities of neural activity in the brain plus its chemical properties make the human brain the most complicated organism in the known universe.' (Edelman's tightly reasoned theory, which follows on from the work of Darwin, has been described as neural Darwinism. Edelman, however, modestly shakes off the compliment.)

Given the breadth of that scenario, it would take a brain of very little imagination to suppose that amid all that complexity there does not exist potential development of brainpower entirely different from its current output. Clearly the brain has untapped capacity. Our evolutionary potential has only just begun. (Ramachandran, in his 2003 Reith Lectures in London, referred to an emergent discipline, evolutionary neuropsychology.) Neurosciences, quantum physics along with other sciences, are poised to transform our world beyond recognition.

QUANTUM PHYSICS

Penrose quotes Bob Wald in *The Large, the Small and the Human Mind*: 'If you really believe in Quantum Mechanics [particle physics] then you cannot take it seriously.' One supposes people said much the same thing when it was suggested the world was round. Physicist Niels Bohr observed: 'Anyone who is not shocked by quantum theory has not understood it.' It is that kind of challenge. Penrose is committed to the creation of an arc of understanding between classical and quantum physics. The scientific world is acutely aware of the need for a unifying theory that would reconcile the two perspectives. Some believe this may not be possible whilst others doggedly stick to a belief that the square peg of the classic model (macro physics) can, somehow, be made to fit the round hole of quantum physics (micro physics). However, it appears most agree that as the two models stand at present the one cannot satisfactorily be used to describe the other. Newtonian law offered a fixed view of reality, deterministic and measurable. Quantum physics disturbs that sense of security leaving the scientific world in a state of flux. Just when we thought Einstein and Newton had tied things up very nicely we appear to have reverted to an ancient Greek period akin to when one scientific law was used for earth and another for heavenly bodies. Penrose observes:

> ...there is indeed something profoundly new to be learned about the physics of our universe at the boundary between the physics of the small and the physics of the large...

In such an arena of uncertainty the door is wide open for undisciplined speculation; enter consciousness, *vis-à-vis* quantum physics. Much is being said about quantum physics to equate it with consciousness, which even to the layman sounds exaggerated. But we are in good company; Niels Bohr gained a distinct impression that quantum particle behaviour is one hundred per cent like human thought patterns. Fortunately, science is not unknown to make profound advancements that arise from a free flow of seemingly undisciplined speculation but which, in fact, turn out to be the process of creative thinking. Einstein himself in his earlier experimentations gave us the first indication that the idea of absolute objective reality in physics is false.

An unsurprising view when we learn that particles when observed behave differently from when they are not. Knowing the question to be naïve, we are, nevertheless, tempted to ask, how can we know how particles behave when not being observed? But we do know that at the moment of observation particles, which were *both* wave and particle (the wave particle duality), become either wave *or* particle. Imagine a dot (the particle) immeasurably smaller than a pinprick having the capacity to expand into a misty cloud (the wave). The cloud is filled with probabilities, one of which is realised upon being observed. The wave collapses into what was a probability but is now the reality, which leads one to ask, are we then an integral part of *that* reality? Surely we are an integral part but not necessarily its creator, as is suggested by many physicists. To state the obvious, the four dimensions (time being the fourth) within which humans exist on this planet govern perceptions of *our* reality. The situation is compounded by the fact that our reality is further conditioned by degrees in individual subjectivities in perceptions. Even so, the perennial question keeps popping up: is there an enabling awareness that links us to another reality, another dimension: a *cosmic* dimension – timelessness? The *cosmic consciousness* event provides the experiential answer.

For the layman reading particle physics it quickly becomes apparent that a distinct parallel exists between the antics of particles in the atom and the complexity of human thought patterns and processes. One could just as well reverse the order and arrive at a description of complexity of particle behaviour by delving into the antics of the neural functioning of the brain.

Correlations with consciousness are endless: particles are capable of huge jumps, missing out 'obvious' stages. How often do our thoughts take a leap forward skipping the normal rational steps – quantum leaps, potentially creative or disastrously reckless? Again, faced with an emergency when driving a vehicle, at the precise split second foot hits brake, the brain will have simultaneously absorbed many options before choosing one of them. Retrospectively, we may not recall those options but they will have been converted into a learning curve for future reference. Or to express it the quantum physics way, a particle when changing its direction (for no apparent reason that physicists are able to figure out) will 'freak out'; that is, become like a cloud touching all potential options simultaneously before settling upon one of them. The residual options that had been explored by the particle may eventually die out whilst traces of others remain to become recycled in other 'transactions' (the learning curve).

In 1935 Erwin Schrodinger published an essay in which he described a conceptual quantum physics problem. He lived to regret it. Yet, capturing the imagination as it does, one is obliged to say something about Schrodinger's infamous mythical cat. It is, perhaps, the most vivid of metaphors within particle physics and probably the most populist image in physics. Schrodinger's cat, it has to be said, upstages TS Eliot's *Macavity the Cat*. Macavity the cat is never there: Schrodinger's cat is everywhere, but like Macavity 'he is the master criminal who can defy the law'. Schrodinger's cat, you see, is both dead *and* alive.

He exists, poor thing, in a sealed box in which radioactive material releases a particle. (We can feel thankful that no cat has ever been put through such indignities.) Just as an electron is both wave *and* particle, the cat is also spread out in a wave through time and space. In that box he is transfixed in a static state. It is only when the box is opened and he is observed (by the experimenter) that the cat becomes definitely dead. Questions are raised. Could it be that the cat spread out in that static state is already poised to perform the decision made by the particle – i.e. in this instance to collapse the cat into a dead state? Was the particle awaiting the arrival of the observer to enable a quantum leap to a link in a chain of events? Hopefully not, as this would be predeterminism – an end to free will.

Many people could be present when the cat box is opened; all would see a cat. He becomes a dead *cat*. Our look does not transpose him into an ant, a chair or a mountain range. It is his *state* that alters, not his substance or structure. Although all things in the universe are in a state of flux, with changes occurring drastically or subtly or imperceptibly, something protects the basic integrity of *things*. But what? That is to say, there is no cause to be carried away by the idea that a *thing* is dependant upon *our* observation to turn it into that particular '*thing*'. Our observations can and do determine our perception, but observation does not necessarily determine reality. What Schrodinger's cat appears to be telling us is that something within us, within the workings of our consciousness (but what?), is interactive with the dimensional world of the particle, connective with our perceived world. Like us, particles 'know' what they are, where they are and where they are going. It is not that humans are the creators of reality – or rather our perceptions of it – but that our consciousness is the facilitator enabling us to discover it. Nothing changes. That has always been the case. However, the minutiae of atomic particles challenge our perspective. We arrive at the boundary between one dimension and another. In nanoseconds such things as exchange of light, heat and sound destroy fragile quantum states allowing the laws of classical physics to apply. Some physicists are content with a reduction to classical physics; others are more interested in the profound implication of those nanoseconds. The smaller the phenomena involved the more intimately intense is the engagement of our consciousness with reality and the less able we are to maintain the illusion of distance. In the case of the fate of Schrodinger's nonsensical cat, he is transformed to a reality state by the look that killed the cat. (Particles react to laboratory apparatus, so why should humans be so surprised to be included?) There does indeed appear to be coherent quantum capacity in the human brain, as there is throughout the universe, and it just might be the answer to the 'But what?' question.

Should quantum coherence be found in the brain of mankind, and to mirror exactly the characteristics of particle behaviour, we are left looking for the sensuous properties; the mysterious ingredients of life on this planet. Particles do not appear to be endowed with sight, sound, colour, taste, touch and smell found in living organisms; faculties that empower a sense of beauty, wonder and awe. Is there, therefore, much more to be learned about the nature and influence of particle 'collapse' into our three-dimensional world? There is, within us, the reach to absorb the beauty of creation that has its roots in our spiritual being. We can, perhaps, postulate that, for example, 'travelling' atoms reach the optical nerve through the retina, which may inspire a poem, a song or symphony. Whatever the answer, scientific discovery, though wholly impartial, has the potential to draw us closer to our spiritual intelligence – our SQ.

Quantum physics begs us to accept consciousness as a potent part of its equation inseparable from creation itself, that is to say consciousness, the entity from which observations emerge. It seems important to make that distinction. To observe is 'to do' – quite a different manifestation from consciousness which 'is'. Consciousness is not only what we do, think, say, write or dream. The intuitive knowledge the *peak cosmic consciousness* experience brings to us is of consciousness as a vast ocean of universal energy upon which, for each individual in our 'real' earth world, emergent activities are kept buoyantly sailing on their way. As we are all well aware, some of our activities in consciousness become submerged, dropping out of sight, out of mind, whilst others rise to the surface to sail the seas, their survival rate in ratio to the toughness of the 'craft'.

Consciousness as a facilitating energy upon which we imprint language, culture and experience, runs contrary to the accepted conception of consciousness in the Western hemisphere. We naturally, and with perfect logic, view consciousness as a highly individual, private possession. Thoughts, feelings, interpretive skills, imagination, a unique set of characteristics and sundry gifts, combine to form individuals uniquely different from each other. Is this an illusion or reality? Both. Human beings are unique but not ultimately separated. What we are as individuals is what we contribute during our life span, but the uniformity of the *peak* experience of consciousness, echoing down through the ages (in spite of the fact that no language medium has been found adequate to express it), informs of a *cosmic* unity where separateness is recognised as an illusion. We would be wrong, foolish even, to ignore the received wisdom from another perception, the key to which is locked into the neural functioning of the brain.

One ventures to suggest that a particle physicist privileged to have experienced a high intensity of *cosmic consciousness* would inevitably conclude that our innate spiritual quotient, SQ, is located in quantum coherence. He/she would have no option. However, quite properly, the scientist will always seek clear, verifiable evidence acceptable to others, but as we have already noted, conventional methods are no longer meaningful. New holistic approaches are called for that can lead to greater maturity and which in turn will enable new perceptions of reality.

Somewhere in the scientific field lies the parallel answer to the profound intuitive knowledge *peak cosmic consciousness* delivers to mankind. It is in *peak cosmic consciousness* that we find the most powerful example of a correlation with quantum physics. The whole experience is a quantum leap into a new, or rather, another reality. Recipients can empathise with Schrodinger's cat for in that instant of illumination they too are 'spaced out', becoming absolutely nothing and absolutely everything all at the same time. In that instant they enter a state of total unity, where in the wave function 'probability' exists – they are both dead *and* alive, but unlike Schrodinger's unfortunate cat they mercifully emerge not dead to this world but alive, re-born and reconnected to another reality. They survive the experience of the Divine Encounter. It marks a new beginning. It feels like a re-birth. They are literally and metaphorically born again in the flesh.

Could it be that this very same divine ecstasy is our companion at the point of death when we shed this mortal flesh? Alive or dead, the reward is one of unity with immortality. The near death experience is well researched among scientists, possibly because it is the only divine encounter in which the recipient is likely to be in a hospital theatre or ward, where reports are more accessible. In NDE there is little or no sense of the body. Going down a tunnel at great speed towards a source of white light with an increasing sense of joy and peace is a common feature of NDE. But unlike *pcc,* the soul may receive a review of what will happen should it return – and there is a choice before they arrive at a point of no return into timelessness. Those who return are changed. They know they have returned to do something positive with the rest of their lives. Schrodinger's cat's time was up, as will ours be one day. Might it require only the 'observer' to connect with outcomes offered by the particle as to whether we live or die? We know what happens when we survive the *peak* of *cosmic consciousness*. Whether the experience is exactly the same when we 'cross over' we do not know. Even so, it would appear near death experiences provide strong indications.

AN INTELLIGENT UNIVERSE

All attempts to explain quantum physics appear absurd because it is profoundly paradoxical. The atomic and sub-atomic world appears to lie outside our perception – or does its outcome lie within it, deep within our consciousness but just out of our reach? Something like a dream that fades even as we struggle to remember? The world of sub-atomic particles is a dynamic flux of energy, as is the state of human consciousness; particles (thoughts) born out of pure waves of energy – invisible worlds of energy. Over these past decades, the world has leapt into a sphere of knowledge so profound we can barely grasp its implications.

Take *tunnelling*. Quantum tunnelling is a term used for when 'weak' particles are found outside what should be a confining barrier. Occasionally an alpha particle (emitted by a radioactive substance) too weak to take a quantum leap will tunnel, not over, not under, not a break through in our conceptual sense, but simply emerge on the other side as if by magic. It is as if when meeting an obstacle, be it a sheet of steel, a brick wall or a mountain, it will spread out into a seeping, permeating mist to gather itself together again on the other side before continuing on its purposeful way. We cannot help but notice that this tunnelling behaviour of the wave particle duality startlingly symbolises the product of our consciousness activities. We are familiar with an image or a thought that emerges out of nowhere, seemingly unconnected with the current train of thought. You find yourself asking, where on earth did that come from?

There is nothing predictable or constant about particle activity. It is a continuous story of fading and constant renewal, particles moving about in greater or lesser quantum clumps of energy states resembling the fragmented mind when thoughts flip and flit from one thing to another. The analogy could be stretched further; the greater the energy state, the higher the level of concentration and creative activity. We might go one step further and say that the state of the universe can be viewed as a vast wave function, which, here on earth, we cause to 'collapse' by acts of observation. For example, within the human brain is a capacity to 'second guess' the secrets of the universe. Heisenberg, one of the greatest physicists of our time, once observed: 'The mathematical structure, that is numerical ratio being the source of harmony in the universe is one of the most momentous discoveries in the history of mankind.' But we must take care, it is all too easy to get carried away. The symbolism consciousness offers us in our effort to understand quantum physics is almost too alluring.

Quantum particles permeate all things. Particles may collapse into wave function – become liquid, solid mass or pure energy – all in response to patterns of relationship and environment. Consider the philosophical and metaphysical implications of the following: twin particles may travel in opposite directions to reach faster than light speeds across vast spatial distances, even across time itself, and remain part of the same system; i.e. they maintain a relationship. By anyone's estimation this is incredible. Einstein himself was very unhappy with what he called 'This spooky action at a distance'. Today, this spookiness is called non-locality, but nothing, as yet, has entered quantum *theory* to account for there being proto conscious properties in sub-atomic particles. Possibly this is because non-local connections appear instantaneous and most physicists continue to insist upon a search for rational, measurable explanations and refuse to countenance speeds that exceed the speed of light. If, then, there is no speed faster than light, is 'an instant' meant to stand outside the universal frame? Or does the instant travel before the speed of light, just as a moving ship travels before the receding horizon? Regrettably, as layman we do not know the right questions to ask, so wide is the gulf between science and us. In the event of quantum coherence found in the human brain we might ask whether we too have a capacity for non-locality. Certainly, *peak cosmic consciousness* provides a powerful pointer in that direction. In that instant of illumination one become absorbed into infinity, you are at one with a *timeless* universe. In this context the concept of time is meaningless. The discipline of physics tells us that light has no mass. Does it in fact permeate all things? In the *peak cosmic conscious* event there is light and it is timeless. Is this where reality exists? Is this the ground of all being? Is it here, in this essence of light, where our ultimate connection lies with the cosmos? *Peak cosmic conscious* people would say, yes to this and *know* it to be true.

The idea that particles communicate instantaneously, whether ten metres or ten billion miles apart, inspired David Bohm, theoretical physicist, to offer a radical alternative solution to speed faster than light that so disturbs many physicists. He likened the universe to a gigantic, magnificently detailed hologram and offered a down-to-earth illustration of a three-dimensional photograph made involving a complex process of laser beams that produce an interference pattern. When the holographic film is developed it looks like a mere swirl of unorganised dark and light lines, but when illuminated by another laser beam it displays a three dimensional image of the photographed object. Miraculously, if that image is then cut in half and again illuminated by a laser beam each half will still be found to retain the entire image of the original. In fact, if that process is repeated many times, each ever-reducing snippet of film, though becoming progressively indistinct, will always be found to contain all the imagery of the original whole.

In the same way Bohm suggests that because we perceive subatomic particles as separate entities we are seeing only a small portion of reality. He suggests particles remain in contact because their separation is an illusion. Given this insight, at a deeper level of reality particles are not separate but become an extension of some fundamental wholeness. Bohm asks us to imagine a fish tank that contains a single fish. There are two television cameras, one directed at the aquarium's front and the other at its side. As you look at each screen you assume you are watching two individual fish. You become aware that, strangely, when one flicks his tail the other does too; when one turns the other turns correspondingly. You might remain completely unaware of the true situation and conclude that the two fish must be instantaneously communicating with one another. The implication of Bohm's assertion is clear. If the apparent separation of particles is an illusion it means that all things in the universe, at its deepest level, are infinitely interconnected: everything interpenetrates everything. There is, he says, an Implicate Order behind our so-called objective reality.

In 1959 Bohm and his research student Yakes Aharonov uncovered quantum inter-connectiveness in quantum physics (known as the AB effect). They demonstrated that in certain circumstances particles 'felt' the presence of neighbouring magnetic fields even though they were travelling in zero magnetic space regions; echoes of Einstein's 'spooky' particles. Bohm, as his holographic model implies, rejects the notion that particles are random and indeterminate. On the contrary, he considers that although particles appear characteristically chaotic they do, in fact, follow precise paths determined not only by *physical* forces but also by what he calls the 'quantum potential'. This quantum potential provides information derived from its environment, 'Like a ship guided by radar signals'. Here, one may deduct from Bohm's perspective, 'the observer' becomes part of the particle's 'environment'.

To date physicists are unable to deal with

momentum and position at the same time. They simply do not know what goes on with particles when apparatus or humans are observing them. All they can do is make models out of predictions of probabilities on a statistical basis. In a profound sense physicists are left to their individual imaginative resources. This will continue to be the case unless it becomes possible to devise apparatus that will not impact upon the behaviour of particles in the laboratory, and this would seem to be an impossible prospect. By their very nature particles are reactive little creatures. For instance, as human beings we behave differently when we know the camera is recording what we do and say. Physicists have not yet worked out how to position a camera without the particles 'knowing' it is there.

Physicists really do face a dilemma. How do they cope with unseen phenomena? (The clothes in your spin-dryer disappear at high velocity spin but you know they are there. Physicists do not have the reassurance of handling the clothes.) A facilitating term 'virtual particles' is used to describe 'unphysical' (weak) particles that borrow a lot of energy and act as intermediaries, for example, electrons and positrons (all particles) enabling them to interact. In the world of physics this is called the Heisenberg Uncertainty Principle, uncertain because virtual particles cannot be seen by the naked eye. Virtual particles, we are told, break the law governing mass energy conservation, but they enter quantum theory because they are needed to describe particle behaviour. You might say virtual particles perform the function of intelligent guesses for physicists enabling them to move on. Virtual particles do the same for particle action. One can see the problem. Small wonder particle physics is at once a deeply frustrating and intensely exciting science.

As we have observed, the human brain is already pre-adapted for the discovery of universal phenomena, deeply inlaid in human intuition. To quote Sir James Jeans, physicist, mathematician and astronomer: 'God is a mathematician, and the universe begins to look more like a great thought than a great machine.' Mathematics and geometric forms exist in time and space. Therefore, they cannot be mere invention of man's creation – the other way around, in fact. Mankind is a product of the universe, the stuff of which stars are made. In his brain is mirrored an evolving knowledge of his universe, a knowledge that is often received intuitively. In a flash of inspiration Einstein realised that gravity is geometry. As Pagels points out: 'Einstein made his conceptual leap far beyond where any experiment could check it before he had supporting evidence. No physicist had even imagined the relation of gravity to geometry.' The world of science is littered with incidences of intuitive activity. Intuition, when aligned with an advanced intellect, as in the case of Einstein and others, becomes a mark of genius. A passage in Plato's *Phaedrus* expresses the following: '…the soul is awe-stricken and shudders at the sight of the beautiful, for he feels that something is evoked in it that was not imparted to it from without by senses but has always been laid down there in a deeply unconscious region.' (As quoted in Wilbur, *Quantum Questions*.) Recipients of the *peak* of *cosmic conscious* could say the same.

However, we were still governed by the 'classical' perspective when those European physicists stumbled upon quantum physics early in the twentieth century. Einstein in Schlipp 1949could say:

> Out yonder there was this huge world, which exists independently of us human beings and which stands before us like a great eternal riddle, at least partially accessible to our inspection.

Whilst many contemporary physicists might agree with that perspective, for others there is a clear paradigm shift. Today, they are more likely, though reluctantly, to paraphrase Albert Einstein with an apology and due deference to the great man – out yonder there is this huge world of which as human beings we are an *integral part* and which *surrounds* us like a great eternal riddle but is at least partially accessible to our inspection. It has taken more than seventy years to make that profound shift, which as the scientific world is aware, begs more questions than it can currently answer. The idea that the world exists out there independently of us, independently of our consciousness, is no longer useful.

HOLISTIC LINKS

As we have seen, David Bohm is one of the few physicists who take a holistic approach to the elusive problems quantum physics poses for human understanding. The experience a physicist has of quantum physics experimentation is subtly different from knowledge gained. This being the case, the need is for greater flexibility in order to move on. Bohm provides an analogy of a stream; a stream with eddies, vortexes, ripples, splashes, etc. Particle physics can be likened to experimentation on those fleeting, transitory manifestations of a flowing stream – all knowledge a staging post where it rests for a while, informing, reflecting, anticipating before dispersal into the flow of the whole. But the temptation is to regard a yield of tantalising incomplete knowledge as some sort of package of knowledge separated from experience. We might use another analogy: Rome exists, we see it registered on maps, numerous references are made to the City of Rome, but if we have not visited Rome it falls outside our experience. Conversely, we catch a whiff of perfume; though it has become part of our experience we may not have knowledge of its source, its existence. We might have imagined it. Scientific discipline would have that unless one has experienced Rome one cannot *know* it exists; that to catch the scent of perfume is not enough without the *fact* of its existence. Incorporating broad implications from experimental data is unscientific and inadmissible. Bohm, however, would wish to make it admissible. He sees knowledge and experience as a single, unifying process.

The Western mind is intellectually and emotionally resistant to this holistic approach. In life in general, and in science in particular, we choose to govern experimentation/procedures in linear fashion; that is, we like set goals, logical progression and measurable ends. We have cast ourselves into a building block mentality; all things are perceived to work together more or less mechanically. Historically, this approach has had its advantages as well as disadvantages. It enabled us to forge ahead uninhibited by negative emotional irrationalism. The downside has left us marooned on our own man-made island of materialism where we find ourselves cut adrift from our spirituality, the most productive of our faculties when used intelligently.

Bohm recognises that that out-moded Cartesian approach – that is, the mechanistic order with which we are all familiar, all things separate, existing (relatively) independently of each other – is no longer tenable. The lesson particle physics is requiring us to absorb is that we must view the parts as abstractions from the whole and be unafraid of intuitive insight, art, poetic language and creative imagination whilst maintaining a firm hold on epistemological data. In other words, Bohm considers it perfectly possible to achieve 'Greater harmony between the left and right brain.' Classical physics too might be regarded as an abstraction of the quantum world of particle physics and not necessarily separated from it. One sees that at last the Western world is inching towards a holistic perspective that has its roots in the Eastern hemisphere. Interestingly, it is science that is leading us into this frame of mind, albeit slowly, tentatively and almost incredulously. Science itself has to face the realisation that some questions are beyond the reach of 'objective reality'.

As recently as 2002 a young Greek physicist, Markopoulou Kalamari, produced a promising and exciting theoretical model of the universe, which by its nature is holistic. Using something called Local Quantum Gravity combined with Roger Penrose's mathematical 'spin networks' discovered imbedded in

LQG, Kalamari produced a structure that becomes progressively complex, eventually evolving naturally into large-scale space. In this model, we are told, space is filled with order out of chaos; an ever fluctuating kaleidoscope of patterns, everything in relationship with everything, echoes of Bohm's 'Implicate Order'. But Kalamari comes up against the usual problem of consciousness. As we noted earlier in quantum physics, i.e. microphysics, everything remains in a limbo of probability until 'collapsed' by an observer. So, where lies causality? Do we go back and back until we find a single observer the other side of the universe creating a chain of cause and effect? When Kalamari asks the question: 'Who looks at the universe?', her answer is: 'We do'. Her idea is that you do not need one painter to paint a picture. One could say her theory incorporates an all-pervasive unitive consciousness. (We recall how in *peak cosmic consciousness* individual consciousness becomes melded into a unitive consciousness.) Crucially, Einstein's light cones enter her model, which ensures that cause precedes effect. The light cone is a mathematical structure that encodes Einstein's causal structure of space-time. It is helpful to think, literally, of two cones placed one on top of the other meeting at point to point. The point is where the event is, the upward direction of the top cone is the future of that event, and the downward direction of the bottom cone is the past of the event. Kalamari imaginatively attaches Einstein's light cones to the nodes of Penrose's spin networks mentioned above. In this way the universe contains observers on the *inside* and causality is preserved. In her model we each occupy an infinitesimal part of the universe. (Note:

This is also the experiential perspective from *cosmic consciousness.*) There is room for individual perspective, she says, but: 'We mostly see the same thing.' Although much has to be verified by laboratory work, Kalamari hopes she has made a viable connection between relativity and quantum physics. She appears to have presented an intriguing model that pushes against the boundaries of current understanding.

David Bohm's philosophy broadly chimes with Kalamari's model, since he also refers to a deeper 'Implicate Order', a self-explanatory term that also expresses the Wholeness of Being. His broad perception is of a vast ocean of waves and frequencies out there containing both matter and consciousness within which human consciousness is 'implicated' in a deeper reality. (Scientists Hoyle and Wickramasingh also view all matter and consciousness on earth as originating from outer space.) One can see how *peak cosmic consciousness* ties in with both Kalamari's model and Bohm's 'Implicate Order'. It is as if they were saying that the entire history of the universe is encoded into the components of quantum coherence within consciousness.

A wholly holistic approach is primed to absorb the intuitive insight the *peak cosmic consciousness* contributes to the totality of man's knowledge. A holistic approach will inevitably narrow the gap that exists between science and our innate spiritual quotient. The current illusionary distinction between physics and metaphysics will be lost. There is a real sense in which physics has already become metaphysical: a word that literally means beyond the study of pure nature, matter and energy.

Perspectives

Have you ever seen a book insect? It is the sort barely visible to the naked eye, making its purposeful way across the page of your book, taking the breath away as one struggles to imagine the size of its minute innards that give it life. We remember it is made up of atoms, each atom containing particles, within which are further particles, within which are still more unknown to us, within which are... human understanding trails off lost in wonderment. And then, when one stops to consider the existence of micro-organisms invisible to the naked eye, having life and movement, one begins to comprehend how far removed from reality is the mind of mortal man. Again, consider the following, if you can:

> Suppose that you could mark the molecules in a glass of water; then pour the contents of the glass into the ocean and stir the latter thoroughly so as to distribute the marked molecules uniformly throughout the seven seas; if then you took a glass of water anywhere out of the ocean, you would find in it about a hundred of your marked molecules. Lord Kelvin.
>
> (As quoted in *What is Life?* Schrodinger)

Just as we are limited in our perception of the inner world of objects and of human life itself, we are equally restricted in our grasp of life beyond our planet. But we should hardly be creatures of earth were we to see all things all the time as oscillating particles. As four-dimensional humans we collapse all we see (including Schrodinger's cat!) into colour, form and shape. Sound too becomes coherent to our human ear.

In this way we absorb the integrity of objects, the sights and sounds of this planet. Science only serves to deepen our sense of privilege and appreciation of this incredibly beautiful world. Knowing about inner layers of 'reality' increases our sense of awe and reinforces our sense of an intelligent universe to which we are profoundly bonded. Knowing that the exquisite beauty of a delicate harebell held in one's hand is filled with atoms connecting it with its environment serves to cement that bond. Knowing that an enfolded mass of measurable sound waves that is a Bach Cantata gives us pause to celebrate the messenger.

The *peak cosmic consciousness* informs us of a developing capacity in the human brain to enter another dimension; we enter another reality filled with an oscillating ether of unspeakable beauty. Accounts offered by respondents to Survey 2003 amply demonstrate this fact. This phenomenon that we have identified as 'cosmic' in character has always been with us. Gnostics, from BC up to the present day, as the life of Edith Walters demonstrates, have traditionally talked only to religion, their voices relentlessly drowned in a cacophony of clamorous diversities. Today, in the third millennium AD, the *peak cosmic consciousness* has something to say to science, its voice as yet a mere whisper. Will it listen? Eastern religion and philosophy are now included in consciousness studies at our major seats of learning, so it has begun to listen.

It is no longer sufficient to rely solely upon the cognitive science of psychology to provide rationalised explanation for *cosmic consciousness* and all its intensities. Its 'discovery' will come as a by-product of hard evidence from neurological exploration with clear empirical data. Regrettably, those physicists who countenance quantum coherence within the human brain do not exactly receive a demonstrable adherence to the principle of objectivity from within their own discipline, but progress draws impetus from opposition, the grit in the oyster.

Physics, in and of itself, is not a positive endorsement of the spiritual; by nature all scientific disciplines are impartial, but for the first time in recent centuries, before they drifted apart in Westernised cultures, physics clearly accommodated the mystical perception. Science and spirituality always were two sides of the same coin, a fact that has been somewhat obscured by aspects of those religious theologies that have little to do with core spiritual values. Faced with the mysterious beauty of the fundamental building blocks of creation, the physicist finds him or herself deeply challenged. Heisenberg, a physicist who believed in the concept of soul and was unafraid to declare it, found it impossible to dismiss religion as an outmoded phase of human consciousness: '...for if we may no longer speak or even think about the wider connections, we are without a compass and hence in danger of losing our way.' (Extract from Wilber.)

Since the time of its founding fathers in the 1920s, the world of particle physics like no other science before it has swivelled us around full circle to face a new undreamt of reality. Groucho Marks, when he uttered the first words recorded on sound movies: 'You ain't seen nuttin' yet!' failed to grasp that as the film began to roll sound was synchronised with action. He thought he was being asked to talk without being filmed. The world is right at the beginning of quantum physics; its dialogue lags behind the action. It can hope to catch up when human beings fully realise that the quantum state that obtains over the whole universe includes human consciousness and its *cosmic* manifestation.

> There are two ways to live your !ife. One is as though nothing is a miracle. The other is as though everything is a miracle.

Albert Einstein

★

Part Two

Survey 2003
Profound Spiritual Experiences

There is a light that shines beyond all things on earth,
beyond us all, beyond the heavens, beyond the highest,
the very highest heavens. This is the Light that shines in
our soul.

Chadogya Upanishad

The Seven Stages of Spirituality

The Seven Stages of Spirituality may be identified as follows:

1) *Innate Spirituality*   Informs the individual at the level of: a) his/her conscience drawn from his/her culture; b) church attendance that may be a habitual observation of a cultural norm, and/or a meaningful allegiance; c) 'God' is exploited for personal or national power and authority.

2) *Innate Spirituality*   Indifference/ambivalence towards 'God matters': Secularised.

3) *Innate Spirituality*   Becomes a *Spiritual Intelligence*: we seek answers. Sometimes these are found in a chosen belief system, usually a religion or a meditation group. (Possibly spiritualism and some paranormal phenomena may be included here?[3])

4) *Innate Spirituality*   Becomes *Spiritual Intelligence*: the

---

[3] Given our current level of understanding in this area, we are not in a position to categorise.

wider picture is addressed. Result: agnosticism or atheism. Here we identify agnosticism and atheism as staging posts, belief systems in their own right.

5) *Innate Spirituality* Becomes *Spiritual Intelligence*: The agnostic and atheist view is questioned. Cosmic awareness may emerge: that 'in my bones' feeling (open to universal sacred values).

6) *Innate Spirituality* Becomes *Cosmic Consciousness*: *Cosmic conscious* awareness is deep and abiding from which spiritual experience(s) may arise, usually confirmatory, but not always (open to universal sacred values).

7) *Innate Spirituality* Becomes *Cosmic Consciousness*: individual awareness gives rise to powerful cosmic experience(s) to a degree where 'knowingness' emerges. For *peak cosmic consciousness – divine light,* doubt is immediately and totally eradicated in adult cases (universal sacred values are embraced).

An individual may pass through six stages, or skip stages before arriving at stage seven, or we may remain fixed at any one stage throughout our entire lives.

★

Comment on the Seven Stages of Spirituality

If we accept Bucke's view of differing levels of spiritual development among individuals, these levels should be present in all world cultures. Here we suggest seven levels. Even in the various branches of Hindu and Buddhist practices we see how ritual, symbolic idols and the powerful intervention of spiritual masters might accommodate people on the first level of our seven stages of spirituality. However, Eastern religions offer a smoother transition, from stage to stage, than the theist traditions such as Islam, Judaism and Christianity since dualistic religions are incompatible with the concept of unity with creation. The oneness of creation is a natural standing ground of *cosmic consciousness*; therefore the seven stages of spirituality apply more clearly in dualistic religions. In all religious cultures and in secular societies, agnosticism and atheism (stage four) is likely to provide a stepping-stone to fresh perspectives.

★

Introduction to Survey 2003

> It is time we shelved our notion of sainthood,
> deifying mortals as if we were meant to be God
> personified. In seeking to elevate humanity to such
> giddy heights, we do ourselves and this magnificent
> creation a disservice. The truth is far more
> commonplace: whilst we walk the face of this Earth
> we will carry no more than a whiff of divinity within
> this mortal shell. It is all we shall ever need.

Right from the onset, I wish to acknowledge that any
competence I may possess in identifying *cosmic
consciousness* events is derived wholly from having
experienced its *peak* intensity. It is not the product of
study or of the usual process of reasoning. Naturally,
the survey attracted an array of experiences that fall
outside a clear *cosmic* category; that is to say, clear as far
as my limited perception can permit. Some of the
respondents' accounts which do not come into my
orbit of understanding may indeed be manifestations of
our *cosmic consciousness*. That being so, it has to be left to
others privileged with greater insight, who will no
doubt follow on from where I have left off, to advance
our understanding in these areas. Indeed, as we have
speculated throughout, it may well be science that will
fulfil this role in the third millennium.

Survey 2003 is a direct follow-up to Dr Bucke's
Survey 1901. His survey included some known
historical figures: Plotinus, William Blake, Honoré de
Balzac, Gautama the Buddha, Jesus the Christ and
poets and writers from across the centuries. In
addition, his survey provided twenty contemporary

accounts of *cosmic consciousness,* mostly confined to Canada. This is a remarkable achievement given the restricted communication means of the day. Two of those accounts are clearly identifiable as *peak cosmic consciousness*[4] subjects. His survey also included an NDE (near death experience) and an *OBE* (out of body experience), neither of which appears to have been recognised as such then. Though Bucke refers to full Brahmic Splendour, he did not specifically explore distinctions that are to be made between the ranges of *cosmic consciousness* intensities.

After a few false technical starts, Survey 2003 spanned approximately a year and ended in July 2003. Links were established with suitable websites on the Internet. Out of the 105 responses 64 were identifiable *cosmic consciousness* experiences (a selection of which are shown in Chapters Five, Six and Seven). Eight responses came from individuals and institutions offering wonderful words of encouragement and excellent information, for which I am grateful. The survey received several long dissertations and many poems, which, regrettably, interesting and inspirational as these are, cannot be featured in a survey without attributing authorship. Survey respondents were assured of complete anonymity. Three negative responses were received (pornographic and a fundamentalist tract). The survey also included beautifully written and moving accounts from schizophrenic people who suffered more from their

---

[4] Maurice Bucke, *Cosmic Consciousness* (see entries: Horace Traubel and CMC)

treatment than from their identified condition. I wish it were appropriate to reproduce them in full, but regrettably it is not. However, two are selected (considerably abbreviated) and the Addendum comments upon psychiatry today. The remainder were accounts of paranormal phenomena. Chapter Eight refers to this area, but because the author does not properly understand them they are not featured strongly in this survey. I am obliged to commit myself to the *cosmic conscious* perspective. I fully acknowledge that many who experience, for example, astral flying, psychokinesis, crop circles and much else, regard these experiences as spiritual. The jury is still out on the paranormal, supernormal and miracles, and I do not have the competence to be on it. All one can do is to join in the speculation.

On pages 125–126 I chart the seven stages of spiritual progression. An individual may travel through six stages, merging one into another, or skip stages before arriving at the seventh or remain in one stage throughout life. Significantly, the content of this survey reflects experiences from people at stages four and over. With a few exceptions, respondents to Survey 2003 did not hold orthodox religious views. The original purpose of this survey was to attract examples of *cosmic conscious* events to confirm its significance within the context of modern times, and also to compliment Part One. I hope this is what has been achieved. The collective noun *cosmic consciousness* covers the many subtle ranges of intensities within the *cosmic consciousness*. Most would recognise its *peak* experience from the descriptive terms chosen from a diversity of religious cultures throughout history: Nirvana, Illumination, Brahmic Splendour; Transfiguration, Enlightenment, Born Again, and so on. In the Avesta, the holy book of the Zoroastrians, 2,500–3,000 years ago, that state of unity was known as Frasho Kereti. All these labelled events, from antiquity to modern times, are identifiably the same event that manifest *cosmic* dimensions within our spiritual quotient – our SQ – and the pinnacle to which it can ascend.

Entering the *peak* of *cosmic consciousness* – divine light (of which Survey 2003 has five examples), recipients become immersed in an all-consuming energy of light and love. There can be no experience more powerful to which man can be exposed and live to survive this mortal shell. As one *pcc* respondent observed:

> We were partaking in God's energy to the limit that our earthly bodies could stand. We were, in a very real sense, a bit of God... we are all 'bits of God' in our usual daily life but mostly we are not aware of that fact.

Looking at a poster in front of his local Chapel: GOD IS LOVE: 'I suddenly realised that the statement is not the rather meaningless bit of Bible speak that I used to think. More a matter of fact.'

On the whole our SQ operates on a subliminal level. This need not surprise us since it is a natural everyday influence; little more than the way we relate to each other with civility and goodwill. Love, as it is said, is 'a many splendoured thing' and is a gift; a gift, it would seem, not confined to humans. Some higher animals display something mightily akin to love, for example elephants' ritual treks to pay 'homage' to the remains of their forebears. We observe also the fine line that is to be drawn between parental love and the survival instinct. Love, in complex forms, may be more universal than we give credit. In humankind it clearly has the capacity to extend beyond self-interest or self-preservation. Love has a capacity to thrive, grow and deepen. Walter Stace, Professor of Philosophy, notes how the mystical consciousness proclaims the secret fountain of all love, human and divine. Human love is all part of our innate spirituality, though very rarely acknowledged as such, even though, in Westernised cultures, most are familiar with the words: 'Love ye one another, even as I have loved you.' Love is the vehicle upon which we approach spiritual awareness, culminating at the point when the SQ becomes aware of its *cosmic* origin. As another respondent put it: 'It may be no more than an "in my bones" feeling but sufficiently arresting to lodge within my consciousness as a defining moment, a whiff of "something other".' Those moments are a gentle reminder, which leaves us with a choice – we take notice or we do not.

Survey 2003 has taken a snapshot within a narrow time frame just long enough to show how much more we need to know about the prevalence of *cosmic consciousness*. On evidence from this survey most people do not talk about their sacred moments, one reason being because that is what they are: sacred. In the words of a respondent: 'To be true to IT, it seems most fitting and honest to remain silent.' Additionally, the subject is still largely taboo. This suggests a whole area of human experience hidden from view under a cloud of confusion and prejudices. Survey 2003 does not claim to match the benefit of focussed research programmes spanning the several years necessary to further our understanding of *cosmic consciousness*, but if this survey has added a little to our appreciation of *cc* and helped us to become more aware of a few of its many degrees of intensity ranging from mild to the ultimate awesome proportion, Survey 2003 will have succeeded, modest though that aim is. One must pause here – that word mild: the power itself is never mild. Our individual spiritual quotient and our earthly dimension filter its expression.

*

Survey 2003

Profound Spiritual Experiences

THE QUESTIONNAIRE

As it appears on www.spiritual-experiences.co.uk

1   **a)** Name and gender; **b)** country where you are living; **c)** brief description of cultural background; **d)** address (optional: postal and/or email)

2   Please say what you do/did for a living. (It will add interest to the survey.)

3   State your age when your experience occurred. (See 12 & 13 below if you have had more than one experience of *peak cosmic consciousness*.)

4   Were you a member of a religious group at the time? Are you now? Yes/No. State briefly the reason for answer.

5   Do you consider yourself to be religious, spiritual, or both?

6   What was your physical and emotional state immediately prior to the experience?

7   Please give a *full account* of the actual experience.

8   Describe your state of mind immediately following the experience.

9   How were you affected subsequently? What impact did it have on your perspective on life?

10   Did you broadcast your experience widely, or did you keep it much to yourself?

11   Are you aware of others in your family line who have undergone the same or similar experience?

12   If applicable, give an account of your other experiences and your age at their occurrence. Use the questionnaire as a guideline if you wish.

13   Do you have childhood memories of profound spiritual experience(s)? Describe them as best you can.

★

Chapter Five

Chart One
Peak Cosmic Consciousness – Divine Light

The following are the distinctive features of *pcc* – divine light within the duration of the event:

1) Consciousness enters another dimension. Timelessness.

2) Light is a predominant feature. Bright, white (ethereal and somehow alive) and sometimes flame as fire is experienced before the arrival of 'white' light.

3) No conception of earthly imagery is present. In addition, there are no human intellectual concepts present from earth. There are no events or 'happenings', no sense of travel but simply an arrival into a unitive state of being.

4) The self becomes dissolved, an indescribable sensation of being 'spaced out', melded into a universal unitive consciousness of indescribable beauty. The 'I' does not possess the whole, the 'whole' possesses the 'I'.

5) Total exposure to an overpowering energy instantly knowable as love. Energy is vibrant with light, love and life.

6) The power of reason is absent. 'You' are not in a position to make deductions, therefore there are no questions only answers.

7) Transformation is instant. Received knowledge of the soul's immortality is indestructible.

★

Peak Cosmic Consciousness – Divine Light Respondents

Numbered responses correlate with Survey 2003 questionnaire.

1,2 & 3: MG/02/f/*pcc*. England. Age forty-seven at time of event. State Registered Nurse. Family background: Secular. Father railwayman, mother clerk. Attended Church of England School.

This account is truly remarkable in that it relates two spiritual experiences blended into one, both extremely powerful in their own right. One would not reasonably expect an individual to receive more than one or the other of these experiences in one lifetime. MG's consciousness first entered the inner dimensions of oscillating particles before reaching their full cosmic dimension in the *peak cosmic consciousness* experience.

4 &5: MG was not a member of a religious group before the event.

I was quite pious until at about fifteen I found myself reciting the Creed and not believing a word of it. Also when singing a psalm which showed an angry and vengeful God, I remember thinking that in that case I was kinder than God, which couldn't be right, so I didn't go again. Most religions that I know anything about seem to have started out from revelations but eventually set into institutions for power, control, hierarchy, career prospects and gorgeous robes. MG adds: *I suppose I see myself as spiritual.*

6: This respondent had gone through a period of great difficulty but was now feeling fit, relieved and fully recovered. The night before the event she had been grieving for those she felt had been hurt by recent events.

I was full of love for them and somehow became full of love for all the people of the world. I realised how wonderful their lives could be if only…

MG fell asleep weeping. Weeks later it occurred to her that her state of mind might have opened up the way for the experience the next morning.

7, An account of the Event: *The event had two parts. The first I can describe to you. I woke up in my bed in the early morning soon after first light, feeling incredibly well (I never feel well in the morning!). I actually said to myself 'I feel WELL'. I sat up and breathed in the beautiful air. I mean that the air felt quite different from any air I had breathed before. It was goodness and energy and clarity and I could feel it filling my lungs and circulating around my body. Not far from the foot of the bed was a table where I kept a tray with glasses on it. Early grey morning light was coming in through the open window and shining on them. I saw that the glasses were sending out little particles of light, which were conscious and joyful, and somehow singing. Each light seemed to dance and sing and to contain in itself all other lights and also the source of all of them. I moved down the bed and sat at the bottom edge. I looked out of the window and everything outside was like the glasses-bricks in the wall opposite, a power cable across the street, torn plastic bags, empty crisp packets… all made of lights, conscious, dancing and singing. I wondered what people would have looked like if there had been any there.*

The second part I cannot describe to you but I can use some words that occurred to me afterwards. Glory. Joy. All. Now. Everything. Everything is Good. Never ending. No such thing as time. No such thing as death. No beginning. No end. I was showered with Blessings, drenched with Love. Such happiness... not just a gentle peace, but full of energy like cartwheels-and-somersaults. Like going home where we all belong and where I was not a separate other thing. All One. All Good. It just IS. I saw no particles, as in the first part, but the implication of their consciousness, joy and constant renewal were all there.

8: Immediately following her experience MG says of her state of mind: *Before this happened I did not know that there was such an experience to be had so when I came back to myself sitting at the foot of the bed, I think I just sat there dazzled, stunned. I really don't remember. I probably made a cup of tea.*

9: *Something had been confirmed. Now that I knew, I didn't know what to do. I thought 'How shall I live now?' I did not make any changes. I carried on with my life as it was.*

But MG sought connections, which she found in a Theosophists' lecture. This triggered readings into Christian, Islamic and Jewish texts and Eastern philosophy, until she reached Richard Feynman and other physicists – Julius Oppenheimer, Niels Bohr, Werner Heisenberg, *et. al.* – making the inevitable connection with particle physics.

So, I don't know how I have changed. I seem to have proceeded in not a very orderly fashion. I try to live in the moment without forgetting to get some food in for the weekend.

10: *I told three friends. They were polite and interested and did not mock me but we soon dropped the subject.*

Her son was polite too.

Such a kind fellow. If ever I mentioned the experience he would smile kindly, nod and say 'Mmm'. However, now that he knows that some physicists are speculating along the same lines he feels more comfortable about his mad mother.

11: No others in family line known to have received the same or similar experience.

12 & 13: No other experiences in childhood or adulthood.

Further Comment: *It seemed to me that I saw and understood everything that had ever been or would be, all at the same time, and that all was well. What I saw was good and the source of itself, constantly there. No doubt. No need for anything else because it was everything. It was a blessing and a gift to me, who somehow had cleared myself, and the light shone straight through, naturally and I became lost in it.* M G added: *Thank you for writing to me. You are the only living person I know of who can understand what I have to say from experience.*

(Without exception, all *pcc* respondents to Survey 2003 knew of no other living person who had received the same event. This was mostly true of people who had received other varying degrees of *cosmic consciousness*.)

★

1,2 & 3: AS/04/m/*pcc*. California, USA. Age thirty-eight at time of event. Doctor in medical research. Has received a national award for his work. Family background: raised in traditional Christian home.

The outstanding feature of this example is its slow onset. No sudden, dramatic impact here but a gradual immersion into the *peak* of *cosmic consciousness*, adding emphasis to its overwhelming power. The recipient, having the setting sun as a point of reference, considers the whole episode could have lasted twenty minutes in total. Other *pcc* respondents to this survey estimate duration in terms of seconds or a few minutes at most.

4 & 5: AS was raised in a religious household where the emphasis was on a God who was demanding and vengeful. Throughout his childhood his relationship with God was a mixture of fear and guilt: *I had very little exposure to other traditions and therefore little chance to explore other thought systems until I entered university.*

This was his first exposure to open free debate among students ready to question everything.

The thoughts of Jean Paul Satre were very much in vogue and by the end of my freshman year I had become atheistic existentialist. Such rapid 'deconversion' was surely facilitated by a strong late adolescent reaction against orthodox religion. I was angry that I had been deceived by my parents and teachers into believing a collection of fairy tales about the existence of an imaginary God that had made my childhood so miserable. The anger gradually faded over the years, but had not quite dissipated when I experienced Cosmic consciousness at age 38.

But by that time religion had no place in my life at all. I was an academic researcher, scientist and materialist. I was not interested in nor was I searching for any sort of transcendent experience. I had no idea what a mystical experience was.

6: *My Cosmic consciousness event occurred unexpectedly while I was alone one evening and watching a particularly beautiful sunset. I was sitting in an easy chair placed next to floor to ceiling windows that faced northwest. The sun was above the horizon and was partially veiled by scattered clouds, so that it was not uncomfortably bright. I had not used marijuana for about a week previously. On the previous evening I probably had wine with dinner; I do not remember the quantity but two glasses would have been typical. Thus, we would not have expected any residual drug effect.*

7, An Account of the Event: *The Cosmic consciousness experience began with some mild tingling in the perineal area, the region behind the genitals and the anus. The feeling was unusual but was neither particularly pleasant not unpleasant. After the initial few minutes, I either ceased to notice the tingling or did not remember it. I then noticed that the level of light in the room as well as that of the sky outside seemed to be increasing slowly. The light seemed to be coming from somewhere, not only from the waning sun. In fact, the sun itself did not give off a strong glare. The light gave the air a bright, thickened quality that slightly obscured perception rather than sharpen it. It soon became extremely bright but the light was not unpleasant.*

Along with the light came an altered mood. I began to feel very good, then still better, then elated. While this was happening, the passage of time seemed to become slower. The brightness, mood elevation, and time slowing all progress altogether. It is difficult to estimate the time period over which these changes occurred, since the sense of time was itself affected. However, there was a feeling of continuous change, rather than a discrete jump or jumps to a new state. Eventually, the sense of time passing stopped entirely. It is difficult to describe this feeling, but perhaps it would be better to say that there was no time. Only the present moment exists. My elation proceeded to an ecstatic state; the intensity of which I had never imagined could be possible. The white light around me merged with the reddish light of the sunset to become one all intense undifferentiated light field. Perception of other things faded. Again, the changes seemed continuous.

At this point, I merged with the light and everything, including myself became one unified whole. There was no separation between myself and the rest of the universe. In fact, to say there was a universe, a self, or any 'thing' would be misleading – it would be an equally correct description to say there was 'nothing' as to say there was 'everything'. To say that subject merged with object might almost be adequate as a description of the entrance into Cosmic consciousness, but during Cosmic consciousness there was neither 'subject' nor 'object'. All words or discursive thinking had stopped and there was no sense of an 'observer' to comment or to categorize what was 'happening' In fact, there were no discrete events to 'happen' – just a timeless, unitary state of being.

8: Cosmic consciousness is impossible to describe, partly because describing involves words and the state is one in which there were no words. My attempts at description here originated from reflecting on Cosmic consciousness soon after it had passed and while there was still some taste of the event remaining. When I was able to think again, the sun had set and I estimate that the event must have lasted about 20 minutes. Immediately *following return to usual consciousness, I cried uncontrollably for about half an hour. I cried both for joy and for sadness, because I knew that my life would never be the same again.*

9: *Perhaps the most significant element of Cosmic consciousness is the absolute knowingness that it involved. This knowingness is a deep understanding that occurs without words. I am certain the universe is one whole and that it is benign and loving at its ground. One important after-effect of Cosmic consciousness that I soon discovered was an ability to create a subtle shift in consciousness. By a quieting myself within, my inner mental chatter almost stopped and I became calm and present centred. Perception of the world and myself were both especially clear. The world seemed benign and 'right' with everything as it was 'supposed to be'. There was a great sense of inner peace. As the years passed since Cosmic consciousness, my ability to attain this state at will has diminished. When it does occur, it seems less profound than previously. I am personally very sad at this loss.*

Cosmic consciousness did not make me into an instant saint or enlightened being. I still occasionally lose my temper, worry, judge people, and need ego support. But from the time immediately following Cosmic consciousness there were lasting personality changes. I do not (usually) strive at living, but truly enjoy it. When I do 'lose it', there is a subtle way in which I can mentally step back and see the real significance (or the lack thereof) of whatever disturbed me. I have not been able to return to Cosmic consciousness, although I have a real longing to do so. However, I can usually recall enough of the experience to know that the world is benign and my ordinary conscious phenomenal experience can only hint at the true nature of reality.

10: AS does not mention whether he spoke with others about his experience but: *From early weeks afterwards, I compared my experience to published accounts of Cosmic consciousness. The comparisons constitute an independent way to stabilize the memory.*

11: Not known whether others in family line experienced same or similar experience.

12 & 13: No other experiences either in adulthood or childhood.

Further Comment: *The benign nature and ground of being with which I was united, was God. However, there is little relation between my experience of God as ground of being and the anthropomorphic God of the Bible. That God is separate from the world and has many human characteristics. 'He' demonstrates, love, anger and vengeance, makes demands, gives rewards, punishes, forgives, etc. God as experienced in Cosmic consciousness is the very ground of 'beingingness' of the universe and has no human characteristics in the usual sense of the word. The universe could no more be separate from God than my body could be separated from its cells. Moreover, the only emotion that I would associate with God is love, but it would be more accurate to say that God is love than God is loving. Again, even characterizing God as love and the ground of being is only a metaphor, but it is the best that I can do to describe an indescribable experience. From the perspective of Cosmic consciousness, questions like, 'What is the purpose of life?' or 'Is there an afterlife?' are not answered because they are not relevant. That is, during Cosmic consciousness ontological questions are fully answered by one's state of being and verbal questions are not to the point.*

(Note: AS, whose account has appeared elsewhere, has granted permission for his account to appear in Survey 2003.)

★

1, 2 & 3: PH/06/f/*pcc*. Wales. Age twenty-nine at time of event. Social Worker (child abuse). Family background: Agnostic upbringing. Given choice to attend Sunday school – chose not to. Father construction foreman, mother ex-school teacher.

This is an account of an immediate immersion into the *peak* of *cosmic consciousness* that was preceded by moments of absolute terror.

4 & 5: *At the onset of my teenage years I came to live near my grandmother's home. My grandmother, Edith Walters, had her own Church having broken away from orthodoxy. Her daughter, my mother, reserved her agnostic position in respect of her mother's teaching and all other religions. I attended my grandmother's church intermittently and was evidently far more influenced by her teachings than I had appreciated at the time. She died when I was age twenty. Many years later I came to believe that Christ's spirit could be born in us but I had no notion of how that could come about. I thought, vaguely, that it was simply a matter of belief, and that was all. I was, therefore, unorthodoxly religious and spiritually attuned.*

6: *One day I was walking along a quiet lane not frequently used by people in our village. I was in a comfortable frame of mind, free flowing, contented, not thinking about anything in particular except, vaguely, what might I get for the children's tea – and the washing on the line – looks a bit like rain –must* *remember to get it in when I get back. Gradually, I became aware that my body was feeling increasingly heavy. My footsteps became laboured until I could go no further. It was as if there was a giant hand laid upon my shoulders weighing me down and pulling me back. I was petrified. I thought I was going to die. I sank to my knees in abject terror. Looking back at that moment I realise I instinctively knew the nature of that death for I cried out, 'Dear God what do you want of me? What must I do?' Underlying this profound personal anguish was a sense of shared sorrow for the whole human race, its fragility, and its suffering. From the depth of my being, I asked to be gathered up into forgiveness.*

7, An Account of the Event: *Immediately, I was in a weightless state, in a timeless space filled with light that defies description – unutterable beauty, unspeakable Joy – Love – Joy, one and the same thing. I want to say I heard the sound of silence; the essence of music but this is because I don't know what words to use to describe the sensations that came into my hearing and sight. Yet, there was no 'I'. 'I' was at once everything and absolutely nothing. Singing Joy! The 'I' was dissolved into a living universe filled with a Living Presence. It was exquisitely awesome and wondrous beyond the capacity of human language to express. A Brahmic Splendour. I knew my soul and other living souls would be here forever. All this knowledge is received intuitively. There is no sense of 'thinking things through', of being in possession of reasoning, of having an ability or wish to ask questions, or even of being in possession of a mind to think at all. There are no questions only answers. Your individual consciousness is absorbed, melded into a stream of consciousness, another dimension in which there is only Purity and Truth and Love and Joy.*

8: *I have little recollection of what happened immediately following the peak of cosmic consciousness. (At that time I had no idea what to call it.) I don't remember how I got home. I do remember entering my home and my husband rising from his chair and exclaiming 'Pearl! Where have you been? What has happened? You look radiant', and I replying simply but ecstatically, 'I have seen God!' My poor dear husband could do nothing but stand there utterly speechless.*

9: *It was some weeks before the afterglow from that illumination finally faded. There followed a period of deep perplexity. So many questions. How was I going to live with it? Where should I go from here? What could I do? Was there anything I should do? Was I alone? I reasoned that since I had experienced this wondrous event there had to be others who had too, but how could one find out? How could I tell anyone? In any case how does one describe the indescribable? I was sure that if I tried people would suspect I was suffering some form of insanity or some delusions of grandeur. For my part I certainly did not doubt my sanity. I had lived through events and circumstances that was the cause of deep personal anguish. I had almost taken my life. Now, on the contrary, I had never felt more together, more secure, more centred in the whole of my young life. The unchangeable sadness that had entered my life would remain but now I knew I could weather it. I 'knew', that whatever life held in store for me there was now a bottomless well of strength to draw upon. You can no longer say 'I believe' you must say 'I know'. I settled down. I would get on with my life and tell no one unless it seemed right to do so.*

10: *In all of forty-four years I told less than a handful of people.*

11: *Yes, my grandmother, Edith Walters, was a peak cosmic conscious person. She lived her life governed by a cosmic conscious state of being, though I was not fully aware of that fact at the time.*

12: *Yes, at age seventeen.* (See 'Presence', Chapter Seven p.199)

13: *None that I can be certain about.*

Further Comment: *One draws strength from the pcc experience not from the effect of waving some magic wand in which the individual is immunised from the worst traits of human nature but the strength comes from an ever developing sense of self awareness and, therefore, a greater exposure to personal responsibility. The strength arises from an active effort to accept yourself for what you are. For some this capacity appears to be a natural acquisition. For others it takes a divine encounter to bring them into that state of mind. For me it would prove a difficult process to say the least. Within that process of self-acceptance one is enabled to accept others. No room for self absorbed introspection. That wondrous gift is an initiation into the collective consciousness of humanity's joys and sorrows within which you are an infinitesimal part. No sense of detachment from the rest of humanity. The opposite is the case. The strength derives from a deep well of compassion for the human condition beginning with your own. No saintly auras present dispensing wisdom from lofty heights, thank God – quite the opposite. Free to make mistakes. Free to laugh, love and cry, one's feet grounded at all times ensuring that we are creatures of this wonderful Earth for the time we have to walk upon it. But always there is a quite little sanctuary to hand into which one can crawl for comfort. Like going home.*

(NB: *I sometimes reflect upon that moment of terror. [Q6] I knew the source of it. What might have happened had I chosen to reject it? I think it highly likely my psychology would have been disturbed for a while but there would have been no penalty. However, the terror was utterly compelling, so there was little or no choice. I did not believe in a punitive, unforgiving God before the pcc event. It was that which had allowed me to survive thus far. After the pcc event I knew there was no place for such negative conceptions within the energy we call God.*)

★

1, 2 & 3: BA/08/f/*pcc* India. (USA citizen) Age thirty-two at time of event. Family background: raised by grandmother in Bavaria, Germany. Most family members killed in Nazi holocaust. Migrated to USA at age nine. Traumatised by this move. Several occupations: realtor, US Army, bus driver, retail management, director of medical programmes, bookshop owner.

This respondent's life from age nine was difficult and lonely with an uncaring mother in a strange country. It triggered an 'escape' into an unhappy teenage marriage. A second marriage brought peace and BA thrived mentally, emotionally and physically. It was then that her cosmic event occurred, which she christened Self-Realisation. There is a distinct hint that objective awareness might have been present during the course of the event, which, if it were true, would lead one to suppose that it was not a case of total illumination. However, we are again up against the language problem. Whichever way we choose to express the inexpressible and whatever the time lapse between the event and its written account, one recognises the salient features of a *peak cosmic conscious* experience.

4 & 5: As a child BA was not indoctrinated into any religion. Later she studied many religions but: *Sensed there was something missing in all of them.*

6: *Physically relaxed – totally. Mind had stopped. I was in a state of 'just being'.*

7, An Account of the Event: *I sat relaxed upon the couch, as countless other times, thoughts stilled, when some happening in the chemistry of elements was altered, for upon me came THE LIGHT; a soft golden pulsating radiance without glare, yet brighter than any colour my senses had ever known; pulsating movements, formless forms radiating ETERNITY. I gazed in boundless penetration within the universe, the vastness that neither ended nor began. All that was, was contained within this timeless, unmoving infinity where all yesterdays, tomorrows, life and death; blended merged into ONE. Thoughtless awareness, more vivid, more potent than sight touched my contained unbounded being, filling it as if it were an empty vessel crying out in thirst. I had become a pinpoint of awareness. I gazed with sightless eyes within the splendour of paradise. In awed fascination this mortal speck beheld the glory of immortality. As the rapture partook of me I became bliss, composed of LOVE and HARMONY. Clearer than the spoken word, THE LIGHT conveyed to my open, yearning senses, the unity of all. No one, no thing was separate, apart, alone. I softened, melted, fused; no space* remained – no me, no you, no them, or they; only ONE. The meaning of life unfolded and I, the speck beheld the shimmering sparks surrounding all that is. The seeds of LOVE and COMPASSION burst within, as a morning flower, their fullness filling my matter less being. Weeping dry tears, I sorrowed in JOY, for the beauty of Being. Out of the vague recesses of my awareness appeared a faint glimmer of duality and fear of departure grew. I cried out into the fullness of the One – not yet – let me remain! Too late, in an infinite blink my mortal eyes beheld once more the world of matter filled with the shadow of dusk. Time duration – educated guess – a few minutes only.

(Note: All capitalisations are those of the respondent.)

8: After the event BA was: *Stunned, yet also elated, full of wonder and awe. Physically my entire body was filled with a gentle 'movement'*.

9: BA understood that death was annihilated and one's immortality realised: *We are all loved unconditionally, saint or sinner. That Divine Presence radically altered my relationship with my fellow human beings… the old values no longer held sway. They had been replaced by more meaningful values… It took years to assimilate even a minute amount of knowledge that was given.*

10: *I did want to announce it to the whole world. I wanted to give others the 'good news'.* However, BA was advised not to reveal it to anyone.

11: *None did.*

12: BA had many *cosmic* experiences following the peak event. Some of these are referred to on page 217 (*Perspectives of the Cosmic Conscious Mind*). In addition:

I had vivid dreams and visions. While sleeping, I would suddenly wake to consciousness and realize that I was awake to my dream or vision; I was an objective observer, while at the same time another 'me' was a participant. These dreams/visions were always acute, yet non-glaring vivid colours and they contained more depth of contrast and greater reality than normal waking consciousness. These dreams/visions contained messages, which were conveyed by scenes of dramatic symbolism. Even now, twenty-five years later, they remain etched into my consciousness. Time and events have proved that most of these visions were prophetic.

13: BA enjoyed a rich and loving relationship with her grandmother in Germany but: *...society felt meaningless, empty and flat – values seemed crazy – purposeless.* Unsurprising, perhaps, in Hitler's Germany. At the same time, as a child, she felt an acute sense of longing and expectation that was to continue into adulthood, when it disappeared after 'Self-Realization'.

Further Comment: For a period of several months after 'Self-Realization' BA experienced the Kundalini phenomenon, vividly described in the Indian Vedic and Trantic texts. Kundalini is an awakening of energy that rids the body of unwanted impurities to release physical energy and a sense of well-being. At its onset, for BA, some of the symptoms were unpleasant, e.g. crawling, itching sensations, hot and cold currents travelling through the body.

At times I questioned my sanity but faith in the authority of 'The Light' sustained me when reasoning tried to pull me into its familiar fold. I entrusted myself to the unwavering certainty of intuition for I recognised it to be superior... I realised a powerful force had taken control of my body... I had never been a particularly active person but now I found myself compelled to be in continuous movement. I was so full of energy I could not remain still. The physical body craved to exert itself, to go beyond its former boundaries. I exercised and danced for hours. I hiked almost daily in the mountains, going mile after mile without fatigue. The energy level was more than my body could contain. It just kept coming. I now know that intuition guided me to this exertion, to this 'load shedding', without this I don't believe the body would have survived.

Note: Gustav Jung has this to say of Kundalini:

> When you succeed in awakening the Kundalini, so that it starts to move out of its mere potentiality, you necessarily start a world which is totally different from our world.

There are those that warn against taking short cuts to Kundalini; that it should not be manipulated by 'exercise'. It is an organic spiritual process governed by our human sympathies and actions towards others; in other words, our innate spiritual quotient. Because Kundalini is barely recognised in Western cultures, its parallel disorders and psychoses may be undiagnosed Kundalini.

★

1, 2 & 3: DF/10/m/*pcc* Canada. Age fourteen at time of event (schoolboy). Family background: farming community. Parents Methodists. Now UK resident. Warehouseman.

Here we come to a case of a fourteen-year-old, which for this reason makes it the most interesting of the survey submissions. For DF it was an experience decidedly tucked away in the back of his mind until, fifty years later, he was moved to respond to Survey 2003. He remembers thinking at the time: 'Is it possible that this light that I became, is what God is?' At the time it was a thought so absurd as to be not worth considering. He was neither an accepting child nor a discerning adult. Retrospectively, DF considers that at fourteen he was not equipped with the vocabulary or mental constructs; the tools needed to deal with an event of such magnitude. It is possible that most young minds are better equipped to absorb a cosmic power of less intensity in order to understand its source. Even more probable, it may be quite irrelevant as to whether the very young understand its significance or not. One touch of divinity and the life is shaped by it, to one degree or another, whether knowingly or unknowingly.

4 & 5: *At age fourteen, I was really very unhappy. My father was – I don't think I'm being unkind or unrealistic – a domestic tyrant. Like a lot of fourteen year olds, I suppose, I had no idea what I wanted to do with my life, but one thing I knew for sure was that I could not stay on the farm. In a desperate attempt to make sense of it all, I read the New Testament, but it didn't seem to say much that was relevant to my situation. At present I am very much interested in the* *expansion of awareness and in personal spiritual growth. But this interest came much later in life after learning to meditate with the Transcendental Meditation people. I have not found any religious institution that is sufficiently inclusive to satisfy me. I am a current member of a spiritual retreat that has no allegiance to any sect or dogma.*

6: *I really don't think that I was thinking anything special, certainly nothing that would act as precursor to what happened next.*

DF was 'mucking out' in the cowshed on his father's farm when he slipped and struck the bony part of the lower leg. The pain was intense, which he thought was out of all proportion to the knock. Normally, he says, he would have hopped about a bit and uttered some rude words: on this occasion it was a soundless prayer, 'Oh God help me!'

7, An Account of the Event: *The instant I thought this prayer an intensely bright light suddenly enveloped me. It was not like a flash of camera which flashes then is no more: this other light became brighter and brighter over two or three seconds and stayed, and at the same time that this was happening I seemed to be dissolved or enveloped in this light. The pain in my leg instantly disappeared with no bruise afterwards. At this point words almost fail me, because my own identity seemed to have been reduced to zero. I became the light, the light became me, and there was no separation. Moreover, this 'dissolving into light' was accompanied by a joy so intense that I've never experienced anything remotely like it ether before or since. Anything in my normal life would be a 100th or a 1000th of what I experienced at that moment. At the same time as I experienced this intense joy, I was no longer* *aware of my surroundings. The stable, myself, the whole world for all I know didn't exist during those minutes. All that existed was this wonderful joy and light.*

8: *I have no idea how long this experience lasted but it must have been at least several minutes. The joy and the light gradually faded, and as it did, I became aware of my surroundings again, much to my disappointment. I definitely did not want to experience again this mundane world. Or maybe I just didn't want to go back to work? As the return to everyday consciousness took place I realised I was no longer in the stables but was standing near the back door of our house. I must have walked seventy metres not aware of having done so. I was standing there confused, trying to make sense of what had happened when my mother came out, looked at me oddly and asked, "What's the matter?" I answered, "Oh... Oh nothing" and turned and went back to my job in the stables.*

9: *The experience didn't make me a better or a happier person, as far as I can tell. But who knows what would have happened without that experience?*

10: *That event when I was fourteen was so odd, so unexplainable – so ineffable – that in fifty years since then I have spoken about it to one or two people, to be received with incomprehension. Revisiting that event again, looking at it from many new angles is like holding a beautiful opal up to the light and seeing colours in it that hadn't been noticed before.*

11: *Not aware of others in family line that received the same or similar experience.*

12 & 13: *None other experience than at age fourteen years.*

★

David Spangler, age Seven Years

This account is not in response to Survey 2003. It is inserted here for two important reasons. One, the age of the recipient is deeply significant, and, two, this glorious event embraces four profound spiritual experiences rolled into one: an OBE (out of body experience), *peak cosmic consciousness* – divine light, revelations and *pcc* – celestial, (that also included a 'presence', a loving silence). It appears the *pcc* – divine light was a momentary occurrence but sufficiently powerful for the realisation of the oneness of creation. The Whole absorbed the 'I'. Before he exited, the soul's journey entered a celestial perspective in which the 'I' possessed the Whole. Chapter six has five examples of the celestial genre where light is not a significant feature.

David Spangler wrote of his experience in his book *Emergence* published in 1984. As a child he lived with his parents in South Africa. He was age seven when this event took place. (David Spangler's account also appears in *Cosmic Consciousness Revisited* by Robert May.)

It is 1952, and I am seven years old. On this particular day my parents and I are driving from the air base of Nouasseur to the nearby city of Casablanca on a shopping expedition. It is a journey we had made many times before, and I am sitting in the back seat of our car idly watching the scenery go by. All at once I am filled with a feeling of energy coursing through my body and a sensation as if I am expanding like a balloon. Before I can think about what is happening, I find myself somehow outside my body but enveloping it. Looking down and in some fashion within at the same time. I see my physical form, my parents and our automobile, tiny objects rapidly shrinking out of view. When they are gone, I am alone in an unbroken field of white light…

In this manner, there began one of the most powerful and important experiences of my life. It came upon me unexpectedly, lasting for what seemed like hours (though in actuality it was only a few seconds), and left me with a different vision of reality than I had before. The experience went through four distinct stages. The first was a feeling of reawakening, as if I had been asleep. What I awakened to was a sense of identity, not as David Spangler, a finite earthly personality, but a pure being, at one with the light around me, at one with creation. Along with this came exhilaration, a feeling of release and joy as boundaries fell away.

Then the light cleared, in a manner of speaking, and I entered a second stage: I could 'see' myself (though an act of visual perception was not quite what was taking place). However, this 'self' that I saw was not a body but a pattern at the center of which I could discern as physical forms, but most of which, as near as I can describe it, appeared as configurations of qualities. In that moment I knew that these were other aspects of me, other lives and experiences that I had had or would likely yet have in what, to my earthly personality, would be the future. At the same time, I had flashes of memories of births and deaths that I had known, and while no particular historical personalities stood out, what did emerge was a clear perception of eternity of the soul and continuity of the self beyond the physical dimension.

To this point, the whole experience was exactly as if I had awakened in a strange but familiar room and was looking around to orientate myself. It was an experience of remembering, of recollecting myself in the purest sense of the word. Once I was oriented, however, conditions changed and I entered the third stage. The pattern of lives, even the surrounding light, all disappeared. In its place I found myself in a state I cannot describe visually except to say that I was embraced by a great presence. In this presence, all things seemed to exist in a profound oneness filled with indescribable love and serenity and with an irresistible power as well.

As if a curtain were drawn aside, I had a visual impression of the universe, a great wheel of stars and galaxies, suffused with a golden glow of billions of suns, floating in a sea of spirit. It was as if I were seeing as this presence saw, and for one instant we were as one. In that instant, it was as if I were one with everything that existed, every atom, every stone, every word, every star, seeing creation not from some great distance but from the inside out as if it were my very body and being. Even more powerful than this perception was the awareness of the flow of creativity throughout everything I saw and the joyous embrace of life and enfoldment in response; the rhythm was that of a ballroom, with music and its dancers and the intricate patterns they created, ever changing, ever unfolding. Then the experience entered its last stage. Swept up by the cosmic dance, so to speak, I found myself looking down at the earth and then upon myself as David. In that instant I felt the intent to be David, the will to be born that had precipitated my current personality and physical life into being. I felt the connectedness of that intent to all the other patterns unfolding in creation and what I can only describe as the rightness of being born. With that came a sensation of great love, not only for David but for all manifestations of human life, for the whole drama and purpose of human existence, for the choice that each soul makes to incarnate and be part of the dance of this particular planet. Then, swept up in the power of that intent and love, I seemed to move forward, and the next I knew, I was back in my body, still staring out the window.

*

Summary of the *PCC* Event – Divine Light

Since this is a survey, one ought to conduct a statistical analysis of what has been surveyed. However, from this tiny sample of five there is much that cannot be deducted, whilst much can be affirmed. The features shown in Chart One, page 136, remain unchanged in whatever age or culture it occurs. Within the *peak* of *cosmic consciousness* – divine light, there is no essential variability other than the duration of the event itself. There are no sights in the normal sensory sense and no travel: there is nowhere else to go. Knowledge is not retrospective but indelibly imprinted during the event. However, this appears to apply only to adults. We have much to learn about its impact upon early adolescents and children. We know the *pcc* event is alive and well in the twenty-first century but we cannot deduct the extent of its incidence in world populations. We have here two men and three women, possibly indicative but not proof of the gender ratio within the whole *pcc* population. One in five having a family history of profound spirituality is interesting, but hardly conclusive evidence of a hereditary factor.

Highly significant, however, is the age ratio. Dr Bucke had suggested an average age ranging between thirty and forty years. He believed that should *pcc* occur before age thirty it would indicate an incremental advancement in its evolutionary journey. Fifty years on from Bucke's 1901 survey the *pcc* event was visited upon a fourteen-year-old boy and a seven year old, which strongly indicates that there have to be other youngsters out there who have profound spiritual experiences. Although David Spangler's account is not part of the survey, we cannot ignore its witness. We now know that we are considerably further advanced on the evolutionary scale than Bucke had thought. Two accounts are evidence enough. In Chapter Seven, pages 193–194 we have two accounts of profound divine encounters experienced by a girl age thirteen and a boy age fourteen. Clearly long-term research is called for.

Without exception, all five *pcc* – divine light respondents were not adherents to Christian orthodoxy. This is true of almost all *cc* intensities. We need not be too surprised by this. The mind has to be cleared of conditioning influences that may inhibit spontaneity. In theist religions – Christianity, Islam and Judaism – there is The Creator (God) and there is His creation; two separate entities, whereas Creation is one intelligent organism. Absolute oneness, unity of the soul in creation, is incompatible with a duality-based theology. The human spirit needs to be free and open to a direct encounter in order to absorb creation's divine energy of love. The knowledge is not that we *become* the universal self but that humans always were *that*. This truth is realized at the moment of illumination. *Cosmic consciousness* events leave the mind independent, cleared of creed and dogma, and replaced with something infinitely sacred.

★

Chapter Six

Peak Cosmic Consciousness – Celestial

Interestingly, Survey 2003 has picked up on a genre differing from *pcc* – divine light. The chart below shows subtle differences between the two. The *pcc* – celestial event is also of another dimension – it is not earth bound. The significance of the experience is not always immediate and may, in fact, remain uncertain for many years. Separation from the rest of creation is understood for what it is: an illusion. This is also the received wisdom of some recipients of *cosmic consciousness* of lesser intensities (which we explore in Chapter Seven).

In the *pcc* – divine light, recipients are enveloped by light to the extreme of our current human capacity to withstand. During the event power of discernment is absent. In *ppc* – celestial, power of discernment may be present but not in the normally understood sense. In its higher intensities, recipients travel through sights of staggering beauty that surpass the eloquence of language to describe adequately. Sometimes darkness is present – an exquisite 'presence', a loving, still silence. It can impress upon the senses as the place before birth.

★

Chart Two
Peak Cosmic Consciousness – Celestial

The following are the distinctive features of *pcc* – celestial during the course of the event:

1) Consciousness enters a cosmic dimension.

2) Light is not a noticeable feature. Profound, exquisite darkness may feature.

3) The body 'dissolves'. The mind is transported. Earthly imagery may be present.

4) Cognition is present in varying degrees, but its normal functioning is bypassed. The 'I' receives knowledge of the whole.

5) A sense of travel is present in varying degrees. Fear or doubt can end the journey.

6) Total exposure to an understanding of an undivided universe – nothing separate.

7) Transformation may not always be instant, but gradual realisation may arrive retrospectively.

★

Peak Cosmic Consciousness – Celestial Respondents

Numbered responses correlate with the Survey 2003 questionnaire.

1, 2 & 3: MM/01/m/*pccc*. France. Age twenty-three at time of event. Designer for TV, theatre and film. editor of magazine. MM is now a spiritual mentor.

Family background: parents 'kindly'. English and raised in the midlands. Attended Sunday school.

Multi-talented and possessed of an adventurous spirit, a traveller by instinct, at age twenty-three MM was already well travelled and in search of life's meaning. Having hitch-hiked across the European continent down into Yugoslavia, Greece, Turkey, Syria, Jordan, Israel and finally into Cyprus, he found what he had been searching for. It turned out to be beyond anything his creative mind could ever have imagined possible. This account is assuredly an example of peak intensity within this genre.

4 & 5: Attended Sunday school but was uninspired: *I grew up considering myself a professional atheist. I was anti God, anti religion, therefore my about face was all the more miraculous when it occurred. It was years before I realised that atheism is as much a conditioned religion of ignorance as any mindless religious fundamentalism. I now travel the world as a mystic and mentor. Not a member of a group or fixed religion as such. Open to universal understanding.*

6: *I was heart and head weary, friendless and fundless at a crossroad in my life. On the third evening in Cyprus, I was sitting gazing vacantly at the sea, when the unbelievable turning point of my life occurred. The sun had gone down, my mind empty. Slowly, a strange feeling crept upon me, as if some ghostly hand was caressing the back of my neck and tingling its way over the top of my head. My skin goose-pimpled and the hairs stood up over my arms.*

7, An Account of the Event: *Then my body seemed to dissolve. Suddenly my consciousness was no longer limited to my body. It rapidly 'expanded' beyond its confines, across the ocean and land and out into space in every direction. Instantaneously, I was aware of being everywhere in the universe at the same time – not only viewing countless things occurring as if seen through the myriad lenses of a fly's eye – but actually felt myself being all those experiences at one and at the same time. The normal functioning of my intellect was completely bypassed by this experience. Yet everything in it appeared to be recorded by my whole being. My cellular memory (whatever the cells were at the moment!) was absorbing the knowledge of countless unknowable things. Suddenly, I understood there was an Omnipresent Consciousness underlying the whole universe. When my egocentric notion of myself had dissolved in That – I was That. When I came to and found myself back in my body again, I realised with awe that we were all That – in the guise of human beings. Life would never be the same again.*

It was as if I had an eye inside every atom (or perhaps an 'I') since whatever 'I' was seemed to look out of everything, every piece of matter, every being (and there were beings other than human 'out there'/'in there'); I was all beings, material and immaterial (that is, beings of finer frequency, not solid); also (when seemingly 'expanding' through the earth awareness) I was fish, trees, birds, insects and all. Beyond earth awareness I was within galaxies exploding/imploding, I was events unfolding (changes in frequencies, energies, movements in the universe, migrations of beings through time.) Everything that was happening was 'me' – not as an awareness of me at the time – but a Universal Consciousness. Knowledge of many things ordinarily unknowable was perceived by whatever was perceiving.

As awareness, 'So this is God!' came to me, by then I must have already dissolved back into individual mind and coming out of it. And in a moment, from some vantage point in space – from one place only – I (as an individual entity again) was seeing 'star beings' hundreds of miles high walking through space, transparent, through which the stars could be seen. (I later thought that perhaps this is how the Greek clairvoyants came to visualise the 'gods' and animals in the stars).

8: *A state of joy – wonder – amazement at the underlying reality beyond the surface of life. I began to return to my body consciousness. The time in that state was eternity. But in biological earth-time it may have lasted no more than 3 minutes. I have no way of calculating, although I recall that the dogs that had come running up to me just before it happened were still fussing around me when I found myself looking out (with physical eyes) from my body once again.*

9: *I had a complete change of diet, automatically falling away from alcohol, tobacco and blood foods such as meat, fish, and eggs.*

10: *I had to keep the event to myself for fear of profaning the experience, although paradoxically I longed to tell, but knowing that even my friends would not understand I kept quiet for about ten years as my own understanding of the experience deepened.*

11: No others in family line known to have received similar or same experiences.

12: No other experiences in adulthood.

13: MM, at age seven or eight experienced an out of body experience.

Further Comment: *The cosmic carpet had been pulled out from under my cocksure student intellect. But a new joy pervaded me: the air was like diamonds on the first day of the world and I could clearly perceive the quality of soul in every being I met. However, I hadn't the remotest idea of what had happened to me. Perhaps I was going mad? I had never taken drugs, nor read spiritual books. I had done no yoga or practiced meditation – thus the awakening was completely out of the blue. I now found myself thrust willy-nilly on what the mystics call the Path. And henceforth there was nowhere else to go.*

(Note: MM whose account has appeared elsewhere has granted permission for his account to be appear in Survey 2003.)

*

1, 2 & 3: FP/03/f/*pccc*. Scotland. Age forty at time of event. Trained as designer. Went into corporation work. Now a body therapist. Family background: (not reported).

FP is the only recipient in this section (*pcc* – celestial) who records having felt pure love during the course of the event.

4 & 5: Not a member of a religious group: *Learned to meditate but do not like to attach myself to any group, including organised religion.*

6: *I couldn't understand it with my thinking brain, but I felt I was being emptied, or some of me was dying. There was no fear, more a resignation that death was near. I just thought I'd better make a will.*

7, An Account of the Event: *I was looking through a smooth conical shape and saw stars being born in a great tumultuous cloud. At the same time I was getting a review of all life on earth (telepathically) to the left of me in a great dusty astronomical cloudy column (in space) and there was a beam of light going through this. This was revealing all the crustaceans, pestilence, wars, civilisations, (I can't remember it all) but I realised that this is perfect. Everything is the way it is meant to be. I realised I was part of the whole. This was all accompanied by purest love. Bliss. It was raining down on me and in me. As I was watching this I went into nothing. But I didn't know it was nothing until I came out of it. My jaw must have dropped, which made my lips make a noise. I was now my lips, moisture, muscle. I am in everything. I knew that whatever I 'saw' I am.*

8: *Awestruck. My brain hadn't caught up with it. In truth I think I was trying to assimilate, somehow, what had happened (but I couldn't).*

9: *I didn't know anything about cosmic consciousness or anything like that then.*

10: *I kept it quiet for about 9 months. Then I chanced to bump into people who knew what I was experiencing.*

11: *I have had a 'consciousness' experience with a sister of mine, but we have not discussed it fully.*

12 & 13: *From an early age I have had the experience of 'seeing' things as a hologram. I would like to add that the experience of cosmic consciousness was a different experience from my holographic experiences.*

(See FP's holographic account on page 234.)

★

1, 2 & 3: PF/05/m/*pccc*. Age thirty at time of event. New England, USA. Construction builder, property manager. Born and raised in Vermont. Adopted.

This is the only account received by the survey in which music triggered the event, or was a contributing factor to the arrival of the experience. As well as travel and sights of great beauty, darkness features, profound and peaceful.

4 & 5: PF was not a member of a religious group before or after the event. Reason: *I have found all religious organisations to be based upon truth but they are unable to practice the true teachings behind their inspiration. Religious or Spiritual? Both.*

6: *Relaxed and in good physical health, I had just arrived in North California – browsing in the local library where I came across a copy of the Tao Te Ching, this was my first time reading this book. Several days later I was lying on the living room floor of the friend's house I was staying with. I was listening to music on their stereo system, which included a very good set of headphones. It was one of my favourite pieces. There are several parts where the vocals build up into a burst of energy like fireworks exploding. Just before one of those parts, with eyes closed, I began imagining looking up into a star filled sky.*

7, An account of the Event: *I was totally absorbed into the music and looking into the imagined star field when suddenly I felt myself, not my body but my awareness, starting to float up into the star field. I started to accelerate faster and faster at incredible speeds. The stars made streaks as I rushed by. I then realized that I was diffusing into and through the star field and that I was also continuously expanding. This continued for some time with ever increasing speed until I was beyond the star field and into total darkness. I could feel myself diffusing and expanding into this dark space until 'I' became nothing. Before I felt 'I' was nothing, however, I felt that I was literally aware of every single thing down to the "smallest grain of sand" as it says in the Bible somewhere. I kept switching my attention back and forth between the two extremes of this divine paradox from 'being nothing' to 'knowing everything in the universe, as in being aware of everything.' Although I was in complete darkness and alone I felt at home, at peace, supported and surrounded by an infinite and eternal nurturance. I thought "this is where you go when you die" then I thought, "this is where you are before you are born." After a while, even though I had no body, I turned my awareness around to face the direction I had come from. Way off in the darkness, light years away, I saw a bluish glimmer of light. It was beautiful and I felt attracted to it. As soon as the attraction arose I found myself instantly transported across those light years of space and floating above a large orangish sphere. I thought it was a planet. I hovered for a while looking at it and then an urge to descend and explore. Again as soon as the desire arose I began to descend, slowly this time. As I was descending I suddenly thought, "I am losing myself. What about my self?" Immediately, with the generation of that thought I was transported back through the star field, back through what felt like billions of light years in a second and back into my body.*

8: *I was very alert and energized and lay there for some time regretting that my fear had ended the experience so soon, even though I felt like I had gone for an eternity.*

PF found the music had stopped when he returned from his experience, which could have been a time span of fifteen to twenty minutes: *...but I don't know for how long it had stopped. It could have been for another hour.*

9: *I was unaware at the time of the significance of the experience. It was not until quite recently, despite years studying many religious traditions and meditation practices, that I have been able to start to realize the true significance of this experience. As I have started writing about my experience and reading the similar experiences of others my entire outlook on life has changed.*

10: *I kept it to myself.*

11: No other family members known to have similar or the same experiences.

12 & 13: No spiritual experiences in adulthood or in childhood: *...just a repeating nightmare of being in a field surrounded by voices descending upon me relentlessly and not being able to make them stop.*

★

1, 2 & 3: IK/07/m/*pccc*. Switzerland. Age nineteen at time of event. Production manager in printing company. Now does German-English translations. Retired. Background: normal English 'upper' working-class family.

Profound spiritual experiences do not discriminate on grounds of disposition. In total contrast to MM/01, we have here an example of a rational, objective mind interested in science and technology. It is what makes this account all the more interesting.

4 & 5: IK was not a member of a religious group at the time of event: *If there were a God he wouldn't want us wasting our time praising him! After the event? A little bit 'scientifically' spiritual, intelligence is behind everything.*

6: *I was standing working on a printing press in a building then situated near St Paul's in London, not thinking about anything in particular, when I became aware of the number of cogs needed in such a printing press. They were turning, gleaming, intermeshing and dripping with oil. I can still see them today. The sight of them must have worked as a trigger, because, and it is impossible to explain what happened, my mind opened up.*

7, An Account of the Event: *I instantly found myself far out in the (our?) solar system, watching, as if quite normal. I could see the planet orbiting the sun, I was watching objectively without emotion or fear of any kind. There was no impression of my bodily form. I was, so to speak, simply a mind with a pair of eyes. It was a magnificent sight. The 'picture' was sharply in focus. I then grew aware of the fact that this was not actually new to me. I knew 'it' was like that. I had known it before. I suddenly knew that I did in fact know everything and it was so simple. Had anyone asked me a question I could have replied, to everything. So simple. And then clearly, overwhelmingly, and this is what 'got' me, I understood that*

173

everything is just one. All is one. The 'aha' experience was quickly followed by a greater 'wave' as the 'oneness' became apparent. Nothing is separate, every single anything belongs to a complete oneness. The oneness was something I viewed from a standpoint nearer to the planets than at the beginning. I remember being so astonished at the way this knowledge was being presented.

8: Immediately following: *I was flabbergasted, speechless and elated. Once understood, the 'vision' quickly dropped away and I was in that room again, as if nothing had happened. There were other people in the room, I looked at them wondering had they noticed anything. But of course not. I don't even know how long it took, a split second, five seconds, ten, maybe a minute? I don't know. I knew I couldn't tell them what had happened to me.*

9: *I knew that something had happened that must have been on a level of a mystical experience. I think I have thought about it every day for the past 45 years. I hoped the experience would repeat itself. It never did. But in itself it was enough and it came at the right time in my life. I know that now. For me, as an understanding gained through life and by observation, I know cause and effect to be the law governing life, whether personal or collective. Somehow I can relate this to that moment. We each are responsible for all that we are, for what we think, say or do. The wonder of it, as well as the joy and awe have stayed with me ever since, although it was not experienced at the time.*

10: *I knew it had been real. It wasn't a chemical or defensive reaction of the brain, as some experts, doctors, psychologists and* *others say, who have never had such a moment but people immediately think that or have similar responses. I tried to tell some people, occasionally, when I thought it would work but it rarely did. In later years I opened up but only a few reacted – mainly those who had noticed life is a little more than being born, consuming and later dying.*

11: No family members known to have similar or same experiences.

12: Dream premonition.

13: No childhood experiences.

Further Comment: *There was no light as is often reported in Near Death Experiences and no feeling of presence. However, the clarity experienced during those moments was more than sufficient for me to know that I was part of it. In addition there was nothing negative about the experience, which is why I talk of 'scientific spirituality'. I had a feeling much later that the scene I witnesses represented something quite natural (nothing 'godly') existing behind everything. I tend to think that mankind has simply become confused and religion has unwittingly succeeded in messing up our ability to comprehend a natural order.*

IK began his search for the existence of God at a very young age, reading such atheistic existentialists as Bertrand Russell and Jean-Paul Sartre, rapidly losing 'solid ground under my feet'. Turning to Buddhism and Hinduism served only to confuse the young IK still further. A loving, caring aunt brought him up during the war years, a devout Jehovah Witness. In spite of 'signs', coincidences and vivid dreams his inner conflict has continued to this day. 'I still cannot commit my self to any particular belief, (I edge towards Buddhism and Rudolf Steiner).'

★

1, 2 & 3: AF/09/f/*pccc*. Indianapolis USA. Age thirty-five at time of event. Artist, painter, illustrator. Family background: Swedish/Irish descent. Middle class. Raised in Catholic family.

In this account there are no celestial sights as such. As we see in the account of MM/01, here too there is complete identification with creation and all its creatures. AF enters a deeper awareness, an 'escalation' of the self into being a presence. The 'I' possesses the Oneness.

4 & 5: Not a member of a religious group at the time of event: *No, religion, in the traditional sense, no longer attracts me. It seems to reflect too limited a view of Truth/God.* Religious or spiritual? *I would have to say spiritual.*

6: *I was physically immersed in the job of caring for horses – cleaning hooves, brushing, etc. Emotionally, I was very at ease. Since Thor was my 'charge' I usually paid more attention to him but I enjoyed other horses as well. One particular day, as I finished grooming Thor, I looked up to find all other horses had quietly lined up in perfect single file as if each was awaiting its turn for a grooming session. I groomed every one of them that day... happy to still be there to see the fall colors glowing in the light of sunset... then I turned to walk back...*

as I did something strange came over me. It was as if an inner voice said, "Don't leave yet. Stay a little longer". This suggestion arose with such a gentle and profound sense of authority that the body just stopped. I turned around and walked back to the horses as if I were a puppet on strings. There was no thought or expectation of anything. I just stood there; empty, as if awaiting some mysterious instruction.

7, An Account of the Event: What 'happened' next is truly impossible to put into words. Suddenly I was aware of seeing beyond myself, from somewhere above and beyond my head. It was immediately apparent that this personality/body had no existence. It was a temporary and substance-less lens that was being looked through. I was simply a focal point as a lens is on a camera... I could see without limitation. Everything I looked at was looking back at me without interference and I knew it to be my own self. Every tree, every leaf, every blade of grass, every hair on every horse, the horses eyes, the sky, the clouds, the birds, the wind, the light and colour... every particle of existence present at that moment was being seen as my self. There was the visual phenomena of different objects but the knowing of no difference, no separate objects. It was my self seeing itself looking back at itself with no differentiation or separation. Then all awareness of objects (my body) personality, horses, trees, sky, etc.) ceased to be and I was aware of only BEING PRESENT... BEING A PRESENCE so vast and so loving, silent, aware, without a shred of desire... and this PRESENCE I knew to be my Self... There was/is no time and no space in this truth, only Oneness in perfect loving silence. This ONENESS is what I AM. This experience could be characterized as having been escalated backwards and upwards, deeper/higher into

MYSELF. During this 'escalation' I was pulled through 'veils' of experience or vision were immediately known to be non-existent, i.e. personality/body, the environment... all were illusionary rungs on a ladder, so to speak, as I was ascending backwards. The most profound aspect of it was that 'I', THIS BEING/PRESENCE, was constant and the same through it all. I'll just get to the point: I AM BEFORE ANYTHING EXISTS AND I AM PRESENT DURING THE EXISTENCE OF EVERYTHING AND I AM PRESENT DURING THE NON-EXISTENCE OF EVERYTHING.

(Note: All capitalisations of words are those of the respondent.)

8: *I cannot convey the truth of this in words and I am always exhausted by the attempts to do so. I felt like an empty shell, a total dim wit and was essentially unaware of what seemed to have happened. It was somewhat like the experience of slowly remembering a dream upon waking up.*

9: *I cannot forget this and it has remained a constant reference point in my life. I cannot believe in this world/myself as reality anymore. I don't understand how the experience of all this is even possible. (I must sound like a lunatic).*

10: *I kept it to myself because it took a long time for it to become available in any sort of coherent form. After about a year and a half I wrote about it briefly and ineptly to a teacher I know. She responded with amazement.*

11: Not aware of other family members that received the same or similar experiences.

12 & 13: Respondent has had other profound spiritual experiences in adulthood and childhood.

Further Comment: AF writes: *I always keep in mind that wonderful Eastern saying; 'Don't mistake the moon for the finger pointing to the moon.' This expresses it (this experience) so well. This whole world and the experience of it is only 'the finger'. Knowing this leaves me mute and in awe.*

AF has won prestigious awards for her paintings. Much of her work is informed by the profound spiritual experience she has reported for Survey 2003.

★

Further Summary of the *PCC* – Divine Light and the Celestial Events

Reading through these accounts one is reminded of the words of Thomas Berry, contemporary American philosopher, cultural historian, visionary and poet: 'In the human it's not so much that we know the universe, but the universe knows itself in us.' What is it that triggers our awareness of our oneness with creation? All ten recipients of the *pcc* event (celestial and divine light) had cleared their minds of preconceived ideas on the meaning of life. Before the event all would have arrived at stage five, six or seven of the seven stages of spirituality. All had, by one route or another, intuitively opened-up via: a powerful emotional need driven by compassion; a passionate intellectual search for 'truth'; coming face-to-face with their vulnerability; having tapped into their deep affinity

179

with the forces of creation or by a combination of all these influences. Music chimes in with all that we are as human beings and is evocative of creation itself. As such, we might include music since it can be spiritually inspiring (PF/05 was listening to music when his journey began). These conditions are the bedrock upon which spiritual spontaneity may flourish. In the last analysis, a deep-seated need, awareness and intuition may be all that is needed to trigger entry into full *cosmic consciousness*.

A variety of physiological changes, at its onset, are reported in six of the ten *pcc* events. They include tingling or 'goose pimple' sensations, (MM/01) and (AS/04); a feeling of well-being – the air fresh and pure, (MG/02); physiological change likened to feeling emptied, as if dying, (FP/03); a free floating serendipity frame of mind followed by a dramatic physiological change – body incapacitated by 'heaviness' – fear, (PH/06); completely open and relaxed, BA/08; a rather comical knock on the shin – physical shock, (DF/10); and in the cases of (PF/05), (IK/07) and (AF/09), each were gripped by a sense of awe and beauty. In seeking a common denominator, possibly the nearest one can arrive at is that all initial conditions were arresting. There was no choice other than to pay attention. Apart from that we leave a more clinical assessment to the neurologist and psychologist.

As we have noted, the *pcc* – divine light is an arrival into a state of bliss where earthly senses are eradicated; no longings, no tears, no sorrow and no objective awareness. Individual identity becomes totally insignificant, lost in a universal consciousness of love and joy. Clearly we have to consider three factors when evaluating accounts of peak spiritual experiences. One fact is known, and that is the difficulty everyone has with words. Language is the only tool we have to describe the indescribable. The very act of using words places a distance between the experience and the experiencer. Very often it is the case that the more we struggle the greater the distance. The second consideration is the time lapse between the event and the act of recording it. For example, in the case of BA/08 it is not entirely clear whether the content of the account contains some reflection on a former frame of mind. Does this indicate a long time lapse? However, in this case it is irrelevant. The 'I' does not absorb the whole. The whole is absorbing the 'I'. This is undoubtedly a *peak cc* – divine light event.

In all cases of *pcc* – celestial the ego remains partially, if not wholly, intact throughout the event. However, we see that 01, 03 and 05 came close to losing the 'I'. (MM/01): 'Everything that was happening was 'me' – not as an awareness of me at the time- but a universal consciousness.' MM demonstrates the highest intensity of *pcc* – celestial. The 'I' is representative of the whole, from deep space down to the creatures of earth. The outcome is one of certain knowledge of the Wholeness of Being, as is the case in *pcc* – divine life. MM became vegan. His newfound affinity with his fellow creatures would not permit consumption of them. It would be tantamount to cannibalism. His certainty about the nature of the event was immediate and joyously received.

(FP/03) says she went into nothing, but the full impact of this 'nothingness' was not realised until after the experience ended. Although FP's account is brief, enough is there to reveal an experience of the highest intensity of *pcc* – celestial. The 'I' did not dominate the entire experience. She received an overview of life on earth and knew that all, in the long-term, was well. All this was revealed to her through a beam of light. When clarification was sought on this point, FP reported that everything else was really dark. She was drenched in love and understood completely that she was both a part and the whole. Having a capacity for holographic vision, FP was already attuned to unusual happenings. However, FP is at pains to emphasise that her ability to see events holographically (see Chapter Eight, page 234) bears no relation to her experience of what we have identified as a *pcc* – celestial event. (PF/05) was able to switch between two levels of awareness; being nothing then inhabiting all things in the universe. In *pcc* – divine light there is no ability to switch between states. 'You' are simultaneously nothing and everything, 'spaced out' throughout the whole event. (Remember Schrodinger's cat, Chapter Four, page 101) PF's account could be mistaken for an *OBE*. In the out of body experience, the 'mind' will often scuttle back into the body at the first sign of fear. However, *OBEs* characteristically hover over their body to view the immediacy of events in the locality of their body and the cognitive ability remains sharply in focus. The *pcc* – celestial, on the other hand, is a journey into the eternal. They become recipients of knowledge of the oneness of creation. (PF/05) was clearly experiencing a *pcc* – celestial event when it was halted by a momentary intrusion of an objective thought. By this time, however, he had already become totally aware of the universal consciousness. He had stayed long enough for the message to be received and understood. He experienced the profound beauty of darkness before his travel took him to a glimmer of light. He had found the place of infinite eternal nurturing. He felt at home in a cradle of love. In the experience of (IK/07) also, once the knowledge of oneness was understood the event dropped away, replaced by 'normality'.

(AM/09) found a Buddhist inner stillness, oneness within her soul. Her reference to travel is in an escalation further into the depth of her being and finding a presence there. The 'celestial' does not feature. The 'I', or rather the *cosmic consciousness* within the 'I', becomes the past, present and future and all living things. In other words, the 'I' becomes the whole; totally opposite to the *pcc* – divine light where the whole absorbs the 'I'. The subtle difference is profound and is no doubt the reason why in some cases of the *pcc* – celestial it takes time to assimilate. The more pronounced the 'I' factor within the event the longer the process of assimilation. When it is finally assimilated, it spells out the same message found in all *pcc* events; nothing is separate, all is one.

★

A NOTE ABOUT DARKNESS

Darkness, for humans, will probably always be mysteriously haunting and strange. We have seen that when filled with a loving presence, darkness is exquisitely beautiful, comforting and loving, but this is not typical of everyone who mentioned darkness in Survey 2003. Where reference to darkness was cryptic or merely suggestive of its presence, these were followed up for clarification. However, in each case, with the exception of (5), respondents found it difficult to engage in words about darkness. (Five is not a survey submission but an account of someone, now deceased, who had been known to the author. It is included here to illustrate the complexity of the 'darkness' experience.)

Responses to darkness:

1) One respondent felt unable to comment about whether darkness was part of her experience or not.

2) 'Darkness and silence – that's all. No fear, just indifference.'

3) 'Abject fear.'

4) 'My third experience… "dark" or "black" experience. I am not happy to describe this without assurances about the nature of whoever reads this… as it could block their future experiences.'

5) 'I went into a void-darkness. I don't know how long I was there. When I returned I felt that all my sins had washed away. I was pure, clean and

perfect. I felt contaminated by this imperfect world. My feet were so pure I did not know how to walk across the carpet. I looked at my hands. How could I touch "filthy Lucre" again?'

It would seem from number five's experience that there are darkness experiences that have nothing to do with *cosmic consciousness*. Clearly, the original frame of mind 'colours' the nature of the darkness and its message. Certainly whatever experience we undergo, from the glorious light of *peak cosmic consciousness* all the way through to the beautiful, profound darkness or to the darkness that is experienced negatively, the 'Holier than Thou' outcome is never too far away.

St John of the Cross provides some 'light' upon the responses shown above in his *The Dark Night of the Soul*, written in the sixteenth century. His is the mystics' answer to darkness.

...the clearer and more obvious divine things are in themselves, the darker and more hidden they are to the soul naturally. The brighter the light the more an owl is blinded; and the more one looks at the brilliant sun, the more the sun darkens the faculty of sight, deprives it and overwhelms it in its weakness. Hence when the divine light of contemplation strikes souls not yet entirely illumined, it causes spiritual darkness.

★

Chapter Seven

This chapter provides examples of *cosmic consciousness* from the near peak experience to the 'in my bones' awareness more common than we might suppose. We have selected examples of similar experiences, grouping them together as we progress through the varying intensities of *cosmic consciousness*. The age shown is the age at which the experience occurred.

*

Cosmic Consciousness – Presence of Light
(5) plus (1) visited in a Dream plus (1) in weak semi-conscious state

This first account has all the appearance of a *pcc* – divine light event. However, there are two missing ingredients, therefore it has to be viewed as a near *pcc* – divine light experience. Unfortunately it was not possible to make contact with this recipient in order to verify the one missing feature found in Chart One. LG does not mention the overwhelming love and joy, which is a constant in the *pcc* – divine light event. It is difficult to see why this would not be commented upon. However, without feedback one cannot arrive at a firm judgement. The other ingredient is a reference in his submission of other experiences that were more ordinary, but just as life changing. Most *pcc* – divine light recipients would say there could be no experience more profound or life changing, but without knowing the full circumstances, or without knowing precisely what the recipient had in mind, it is unsafe to draw conclusions.

LG/015/m/cc. England. Age thirty-five

I was in what seemed a normal night's sleep, when I was awoken by a powerful sensation that I cannot describe, and found myself surrounded by the brightest light. I would say the nearest colour would be gold but that does not describe it. I no longer seemed solid but made of the same air or liquid as the light. My thoughts were by way of nothing, just oneness. After the event: It was rather like a shock but not involving fear, with a sense of newness. It made me seek at every level, and realise, for me that the deeper meaning of this life is the development of our soul.

LG was not a member of a religious group before the event. He has now discovered the value of meditation and living in the 'now'.

★

PH/018/f/cc USA. Age twenty-six

I was lying on my couch in the living room of my apartment. I was tired and depressed. I had a one-year-old baby napping upstairs, an unhappy marriage and a lot of responsibilities that had overwhelmed me. I prayed for help and guidance and heard my baby wake up and start to cry. I just didn't have the energy to go pick him up and I prayed, "God, please help me, I am so tired and sad. Please help me for the sake of my son whom I love so much. I know that you understand because you had a son you loved too". Suddenly the room was filled with golden, buoyant light. I stood up and felt that it enveloped me and that it almost held me up, as though I were surrounded by something more physical than just light. At the same time I also felt the heavy weight of depression lift and I knew with total certainty that there was a God and that he was there for me. The thought formed in my head that I didn't have to struggle alone and that I never had had to. I cannot truly describe the peace, happiness, relief and love that I felt. I also felt that everything was truly alright with the world on some level. It's really hard to explain. This happened in a few minutes I think. I went to the window when the light had faded to see if the curtains were open a little, but it was just another cold, grey Ohio afternoon in the winter. I knew that it wasn't sunlight but I had to check. I wrote my grandmother about my experience and she copied my letter and sent it back. I am glad she did as I still have a written account of what happened that day. She knew it was an important event in my life. I have never forgotten it and never doubted the existence of God since then. I still struggle with depression but I know that if I feel a distance between myself and God it is I who have moved and not God. I know that sounds trite, but it is true.

PH told no one only her grandmother. This respondent was not a member of a religious group before or after the event.

★

AD/021/f/cc. England. Age not known

After much messing about and to-ing and fro-ing from hospital, I was eventually given four pints of blood and, later operated upon. Leading up to this, my consciousness was drifting away in waves; my attachment to my body became more and more tenuous. Getting closer to the operation, it became more and more unpleasant as there was hustle and bustle around me. At one point, in desperation, I lifted my inner 'eye' /mind, upwards, thinking very purposefully of Jesus. I was immediately aware of a sphere above me, taking the origin of direction from inside my mind. This sphere did not have sharply defined boundaries. It spread out from a very concentrated centre, and it was of light, radiant and steady and uplifting, and it was of love... warm, nourishing, like a blessing and a bathing. It was significant to have fallen upon this source of help. It felt like a consciousness and I thought of it as my Guardian Angel; without doubt it was a very real Presence there for me to call upon according to need.

This respondent had a difficult and lonely childhood that included threats of sexual abuse from a stepfather. Brought up in an environment hostile to religious thought, AD found solace and meaningful comfort in Jesus the Christ that continued into adulthood until another profound experience led her to find an all inclusive Tibetan philosophy (see Revelation, page 197).

★

NB/022/m/cc. USA. Mexican/American

I was a runaway at age seventeen. Most of my siblings also left home very young. I had a brother I had not seen in seventeen years and I was tracked down by UC San Diego Doctors. My brother was dying of leukaemia and they needed me to test whether I could do a bone marrow transplant. I was a perfect match. I did the bone marrow and reconnected with my brother. He relapsed two years later and I did several other

189

transplants to try save his life. During one of our last transplants, it was understood that there was nothing else to do. One night I experienced the Holy Spirit. In my dream it touched my head – I could not see any real figure, other than a large golden light. When the light touched me, I felt the most love I have ever felt and it was overwhelming. The light messaged to me that I was a blessed child. I was then on my knees praying to the light that was before me and I woke up crying – not from sadness – but from an overwhelming joy. That night I phoned my brother – who was not sleeping anymore, as he knew he was going to die soon. My brother that night also experienced something – three angels coming into his room and blessed him. Two years later, angels appeared in my dream contacting me and I visited heaven. I thought of my brother and the experience he went through. I have a much larger view of our purpose on earth and what life on earth provides.

NB is an activist for the poor and under-served. Non-religious. Says he is 'spiritual'.

★

ADW/024/m/cc. Wales. Age twenty-three

I was lonely and upset, practising yoga, reading what little I could find. Rather horrified to be in active part of war on a large ship during the Korean campaign. I was just leaving the ship, stepping onto the gangplank to go ashore in Japan. I became aware that the nature of the world had changed; it was glowing. I was uplifted in spirit and wandered round the Japanese port in that exalted state of mind. The experience was intense for several hours and the 'afterglow' was strong for about three days. I felt a strong sense of love – an undifferentiated general feeling. It confirmed my feeling that one might experience a different, more spiritual, life.

ADW is now a member of a Buddhist group.

★

CJ/025/m/cc. England. Age thirty-three

Hyperventilation reached critical and certain parts of my body began to recede. A warmth and a brilliant white light began to grow. It felt like 'coming home'. My state of consciousness was undoubtedly altered. Glad to be alive but sad to lose the light. It's sort of reassuring to have partially experienced the 'all one'. I tell anyone who listens. Non-religious before and after the event.

CJ says he is: '*As spiritual as my cat*'!

★

NOP/026/f/cc. USA. Age thirty-eight

I was at a workshop when I felt the presence of 'God'. There was a white light illuminating everyone in the room (about 50) it seemed to be protecting and caring and loving everyone as they practiced breathing. I was totally awe struck.

NOP was not a member of a religious group before or after the event.

★

THE INDIAN TANTRIC WAY (1)

This experience might be called the Indian Tantric Way. It is a beautiful account of earthly lovers who blend their beings one with the other in perfect union and where loving ecstasy melds into divine ecstasy. The soul, no longer conscious of the body, enters a state of oneness with creation. The profound symbolism of sexual love and divine love is well expressed in art, poetry and literature throughout the ages. In Part One we identified our SQ, our spiritual quotient, as a vehicle for love in all its many splendoured forms: 'There is a divinity that shapes our ends. Rough-hew them how we will' (Shakespeare, *Hamlet*). Many experiences in life have the power to bring us closer to *cosmic* awareness; the miracle of birth is one such obvious event. The miracle of love between a man and a woman is another. Survey 2003 is privileged to receive this account.

PS/027/m/cc. England. Age twenty-seven

I was on a quest to find truth, the meaning of life, for around 10 years. This culminated in lots of thinking, self-understanding, leading to philosophy and meditation. I went to India where this became very concentrated, sustained process. In the few days leading to the experience I read, thought and wrote a lot about sub-atomic physics, and then, whilst making love with my partner I felt a melting, surging warmth around my groin and abdomen which rose to my chest. On looking down I realised myself and my partner had merged as one. This sublime sensation continued to rise in my body as I became aware of my breathing becoming suspended. I went into this suspension and felt myself to have a choice, to leap into the unknown, beyond all previously experienced reality, or pull back from the experience, the swell of love subtly and most profoundly burst through my mind in ecstatic bliss, oneness, unity, suspended outside time, boundless, no separation, me, everything, one. For the next few days my awareness and energy were a loving delight. I had experienced God. I am God's child, of God, God touched me, enlightened me, I had found the meaning of life. Love. I realised my oneness with all living beings and the miraculous nature of life. My consciousness shifted. My ego became quite transparent. I stopped owning thoughts. I now considered myself to be a spiritual person. I do not consider any one religion/group to have the monopoly of spiritual truth.

PS felt compelled to share his experience with chosen others but found them unappreciative. After a while he kept it to himself unless asked by people with a genuine interest.

★

ONENESS WITH CREATION (3)

GG/030/f/cc. UK. Age thirteen

I was looking out of a kitchen window. Suddenly, there was no separation between the entire universe and me. There was no separate me. I was everything and everything was part of me. I was conscious of the grass on the lawn that I was looking at, that I was also every blade of that grass, there was no separation between me and everything in existence. I realised separation was an illusion. This state of consciousness blew me away. I was stunned and exhilarated. I had had no idea that everything I had believed was wrong. I could no longer look at the world in the same way. I soon realised that if I told my parents or friends they would think I was mad. Also I had no way of expressing properly what had happened. I was worried that maybe there was no one else who knew what I knew.

What if I was the only person in the world that this had happened to? I kept it a secret for many years. I am much less religious now than before the original experience.

It will be noted that this remarkable event experienced by a thirteen-year-old has similarities with accounts found in *pcc* – celestial. Indeed the only missing feature is travel. It was nevertheless a near-peak experience, as is the account of the fourteen-year-old boy below.

★

JMK/031/m/cc. Scotland. Age fourteen. Brought up on a Hebridean island

I was standing at a window looking out over a field to the sea, feeling rather detached and calm. A feeling suddenly swept over me that I was physically connected to the landscape in front of me, and through it to the whole earth, as if it and I were made of the same substance. The landscape seemed to be ablaze with significance and to glow, although the colours I saw did not change. At the same time I was aware that all the evil and good in the world were part of it too and were really the same thing and did not need to be distinguished from each other, just as the hills and valleys in a landscape become indistinguishable when viewed from an aeroplane (this metaphor occurred to me at the time, or rather, was part of the feeling). I knew that whatever happened to me or to anyone else everything would be for the best in the end. I have no way of telling how long this experience lasted for, but I imagine it was about a minute or so. I felt exalted, uplifted and at peace but sad that the experience had ended. I discussed the experience with a few friends.

Here again we have a fourteen-year-old receiving

profound insights, which one would normally consider to be in advance of his age. The presence of glowing colours is deeply significant.

Subsequently, I have always enjoyed a deep down feeling of confidence that everything will in fact be for the best even if on the surface I was dissatisfied or unhappy.

Not religious before or after the event, JMK says he has an antipathy to dogma and organised religion. Later in life JMK experimented with drugs and had a powerful but dissimilar episode: *However, I now believe that drugs are a blind alley.*

★

NOP/033/f/cc. USA Age thirty-six

As I drove back from Tallahassee, I started feeling odd and pulled off the road. As I did the view became frighteningly clear – as clear as the view becomes when one tries out new lens prescription for nearsightedness. I was awestruck. It seemed that I could see individual leaves and blades of grass far away – a great sense of peace and also of excitement and the feeling that I was not alone that a large spirit surrounded me. I felt sincerely grateful.

NOP was Presbyterian before event. Not religious now.

How many manifestations are there of God? I don't know or care. It's all one and everything leads back to the same place.

★

PARTICLE ENERGY (1)

Experiential data tell us that somewhere within the incredible complexity of the human brain is a capacity to connect with the inner dimension of the particle. We should not be surprised by this since we are composed of atoms, as is everything else in the known universe. Below we have a Fritjof Capra like experience. (Capra, Particle Physicist, tells of his own experience of 'dancing particles' in *The Tao of Physics*.)

MS/034/m/cc. Australia. Age forty-five at time of event. Atheist

My partner decided to end our relationship. I had no money whatever. I was stony broke and absolutely at the lowest point in my life. I had lost faith in everything. I lived in a small village in the bush. One day walking the dogs I was in total despair. I sat down on a log and put my head in my hands and from the bottom of my heart. "What's it all about? I don't understand." For a while nothing happened, I sat totally open to whatever. What happened next has stayed with me. The first sensation was an incredible feeling coming up from my feet to gradually encompass my entire body. The nearest sensation that I can relate it to is an intense orgasm – but still being aware of what is going on. As my eyes were closed at the time, I thought I would open them just to see it things looked different. I wasn't expecting to see what I did. Every single blade of grass, stone or tree looked as if it had energy of its own, as though there was light in it, some kind of inner energy. This didn't last very long. I stood up, the feeling inside had lost its intensity. I felt so calm, at peace, just a feeling of sublime bliss entirely within me. As I was standing there trying to figure out what had just happened to me, I then heard/felt a voice inside my chest area quite firmly say: 'Don't worry. Nothing matters.' I honestly didn't know what to make of it. I thought I might be having some kind of a nervous relapse. At the time I was an atheist and later believed it was like energy from the earth or nature to revive me. Ever since that experience I am a lot more relaxed and not concerned about material things or money, nor position. I seemed to live a charmed life as long as I didn't try too hard to achieve things, then I would start seeing adverse things in my life. I know there is some kind of energy that exists that science cannot measure yet, but one day will, and we are getting very close. There is a lot more to the mind that is not understood and we can't readily tap into yet. With us using only a small percentage of our brain it doesn't mean we can't.

(See also MG/02, Particle Energy, page 137)

MS found another person who understood his experience completely.

★

REVELATION

AD/035/f/cc *(Revelation)*. England. Age thirty-eight

I was under anaesthetic. Various things were registered by my conscious mind during this time (the fallopian tube had burst six days previously, so it was truly a miracle that I was alive at all). At some point I was aware that I was a 'consciousness', that I did not have the normal limitations to my identity or being, that I could expand my consciousness, or reduce it, according to whim. There was no body clinging. Then I experienced a great rushing airy presence of indescribable power and vitality and joy. It was enormous; I do not know how to describe its enormity. I had no means to define its boundaries. The sense of power did not frighten me. The sense of vitality was reassuring; the sense was that life could not end; this vitality was the essence of life and could not be destroyed. But it could change its shape even though it always remained an essence, the spirit of life, and this spirit did change its shape continuously and joyously and playfully. It flowed in and out of forms, picking then up and casting them away without a shred of loss when they had outworn their purpose. This aspect of the revelation was of an abundance of joy in the experience of life. Nothing could diminish this joy. It revealed that the forms themselves possessed no life of their own… they had life in as much as they were filled with this spirit, which itself was not divided. It was oneness everywhere. It is difficult to encapsulate in words the understanding and insight that was revealed to me by this vision… sorry, not a 'vision' because it was not seen it was experienced in the essence of my being. Afterwards I felt re-born and that I had been given the gift of life. My revelation had shown me that I could never shut off or end that essential spirit itself. And that spirit, being impelled ultimately from the One Spirit or Divine Life, would anyway return through another garment, or body, to continue its exploration in its chosen way. I knew beyond debate, beyond question that God existed. But I also recognise that it was enough for me to know this. There was no need for me to tell anyone else what I knew or try to influence their views. After this experience I actively sought to find a religious discipline that I found acceptable. I found the teachings of the Tibetan Master Dhwhal Khul fully inclusive and meaningful to all world religious followers and not claiming to be necessarily the only truth.

(NB: this account might be taken as an *OBE* by some expert researchers, since some *OB*'s inhabit shapeless clouds of energy under anaesthetic. AD/035 is included here for the revelation of knowledge, joy, love and oneness. In addition AD was left with a newfound security and a sure sense of personal renewal.)

★

PRESENCE (1)

PH/036/f/cc. Wales. Age seventeen

I was on a bus returning from a singing lesson feeling relaxed and happy. Gradually I felt surrounded by a loving aura that absorbed all my attention. (No light). I became totally unaware of my surroundings. Then out of this Presence I heard a beautiful voice say quite simply: You are a child of God. Then the Presence faded leaving me peaceful and content. Strangely, I did not think it strange since I had already accepted the idea that we were all sons and daughters of God. Even so, I knew perfectly well that I should keep it to my self. I dared not tell anyone. It was after all a very private communion and I decided that it might cause my mother a problem. I felt loved and protected for a long time afterwards. Agnostic parental background. I attended my grandmother's church intermittently. [See Edith Walters, Chapter One.]

★

COLLECTIVE CONSCIOUSNESS (1)

Gustav Jung's work on the collective conscious points out the attributes of collective consciousness, in which there is an awareness of being part and parcel of the whole that results in individuals developing a more holistic view of humanity. An inexplicable wave of deep sadness for the plight of others in the world is a common enough phenomenon. These feelings may arrive out of the blue even when relaxed, calm and peaceful. Though not directly related to one's personal life or family, the pain is real and physical. One becomes acutely aware of the suffering in the world. It is guaranteed that always someone somewhere, at this moment is suffering. In today's world, immediate and graphic images of untold suffering the world over can be seen almost daily on our television screens or heard on the radio. Whether we relate our personal pain of awareness to this or that event is almost irrelevant. There is always more than enough pain to go around. We have here a classic example of how colossal tragedy releases the power of love. Compelling, productive, pro-active and counterbalancing, compassion is never wasted.

SLP/038/f/cc. California. Age forty-six

Account. September 11, 2001, 4 a.m. PDT

September 11 is my birthday. I turned forty-six. I woke up at 4:00 with an overwhelming sense of sadness and loss. It was so powerful I woke my husband to tell him about it. I was having trouble explaining the feelings and where they were coming from. I said "You know in 'Amazonia' by Neil Young, Harvest Moon album, how he talks about the beauty of the young cowgirls & Chevrolets at the rodeo and how they won't realize how beautiful they are until their beauty is gone. It's tied to the loss of the Amazon." I couldn't finish because I started sobbing uncontrollably. I sobbed for hours. My poor husband thought I was mad at him. I was shocked at myself because it's not like me to be upset because I'm growing older. I like growing older. The whole thing was very confusing. The emotions came from somewhere outside myself. I was crying for the world, if that makes sense. I was finally able to doze around 6:00am. Our clock radio alarm went off at 7:00am. News of the WTC bombing was on the radio. I went into shock. My husband called work and said I wouldn't be in. Around 12:00 I got dressed and decided to snap out of it. I was very calm and centred all day. I now know, without doubt that I am capable of connecting with the collective consciousness. I started noticing how people turn to me as teacher and guide in all sorts of situations. My view of myself as clueless is not the way the world sees me. I've taken this to heart and accepted the honour they give me along with the responsibilities it entails. I know my role is to help people, to be calm, loving and compassionate and to help them negotiate through difficult times with their best selves.

SLP is a non-churchgoer: '*I have deep religious beliefs. I just try to live them.*'

★

EXTENDED *COSMIC CONSCIOUSNESS* (2)

JT/040/m/cc. England. Age twenty-six

My state of bliss lasted around three months when I had become like a child with a new fascination in the world around me. It changed my life in that I came to see what was important in life… it developed in me a kindness towards strangers and having the patience to really listen to what people are saying.

★

RH/041/m/cc. Ireland. Age twenty-eight

For a whole week I was in contact with the absolute. Meaning that while I would go about my life in the usual way, I had this strange kind of perspective beyond our relative world. It is very difficult to describe. It proved to me beyond all doubt that something else exists outside us as perceived in the here and now, something eternal. At the time I did not understand where this experience was coming from, even though I was doing meditation and practicing Ki Aikido, a spiritual martial art. Then I remembered that three months before I had asked the question in meditation: Is there something outside us? This was the answer.

RH was not a member of a religious group before the experience, but now: *Yes, I enjoy an open religious community.* RH does not name the religion.

★

RECOGNITION OF THE DIVINE IN OTHERS (2)

BK/9044/f/cc. England. Age 28

I was doing a walking meditation indoors, another participant who was dirty and smelly was walking in the opposite direction to me around the room, so we had to get out of each other's way, which was very distracting. On one circuit, he bent down and moved a stool out of my path. I experienced a change of state of consciousness and was 'at one' with the

Divine in this other person. I didn't know, or feel, or think – it just was- there was only one. Which was love. When I came back to reality I was on my knees weeping for all the times I had judged people/failed to recognise that we are all one.

The experience has significantly caused BK to change her treatment of herself and others.

I try to be aware at all times (as the Quakers say) that 'There is that of God in everyone.'

★

GG/046/f/cc. England. Age not known

I was in Switzerland; I was arriving at a house when someone I knew met me in the entrance hall. I looked into her eyes and something happened. I had seen the divine in others eyes before, but not like this. This was so mind blowing that I still haven't integrated the experience. At the time I just said hello and walked on.

★

THE HEM OF HIS GARMENT (7)

Those moments in life when we are alerted to 'something other', divine energy – call it what we will – are too numerous to enumerate. They touch every aspect of our lives in music, art, an overheard conversation, a child's smile; they can be deeply personal and solitary moments or something shared with others. Below is a selection of experiences that are just a little more than 'in my bones' feelings. The last entry in this section is, in fact, an example of 'in my bones' feeling most will recognise.

BF/048/m/cc. England. Age thirty-four

I was in a calm and peaceful state of mind when I felt as if I was in a sort of cosmic shower and in deep communion with the Christian version of God. Afterwards I was exhilarated. Definitely not religious.

This appears to be a contradiction in terms unless BF is referring only to the inspiration of Christ's doctrine of love.

★

TW/049/m/cc. Wales. Age twenty-eight

For many years I had been asking the question about what to do with my life. Was there any God or even a spiritual entity? One morning I woke and the only thing in my head were the words "Be still and know that I am God." I looked it up in the printed word but it had no meaning – only the voice in my head.

TW was a member of a religious group. Still feels he is religious with a small 'r'.

★

AW/050/f/cc. England. Age fifty-two

The occasion happened in Bedgellert (Wales) where my husband and I were on holiday. I approached a stream and suddenly I felt that I was in another country. The colours seemed brighter and the world seemed a more beautiful place

(Bedgellert is beautiful anyway). I had a wonderful feeling of peace. I felt connected with the universe but the experience did not profoundly change my life. Our only son died suddenly and I suppose I began looking for answers. No religion fits in with my philosophy.

★

HM/051/f/cc. England. Age twenty-seven

I was at rest, neutral. There was a commonality of thought and understanding in the Meeting (Quaker) – almost a physical feeling of something moving around the Meeting in a circle from person to person.

HM continues her membership of the Quaker Society.

★

PH/053/f/cc. Wales. Age seventy-one

I woke up one morning. Sat up, alert, expectant. I heard a voice. It spoke just one word – my name – so clear, so beautiful but gently reproving. I knew at once what it meant. I had lapsed for too long in the middle of a project I knew I had to complete. So I got on with it! It was the writing of this book.

★

SH/054/f/cc. Wales. Age forty-five

For several weeks I had been feeling depressed and listless and not coping well at work. I could find no good reason for it. Everything seemed OK in my life. Why was I so depressed? I went into a meditative frame of mind, sinking down deep, asking for help. Very quickly I began to feel better. Several weeks later it dawned on me – how could I have been so stupid? I worked it out – I hadn't had a menstrual period for over three months. I had suddenly stopped, my body deprived of essential hormones. I visited the doctor who prescribed HRT. Up until then I had not heard of hormone replacement therapy. I know that during that period of hormonal deprivation I had received help. It had been a case of mind over matter.

★

PW/055/f/cc. Scotland. Age fifty

We were travelling on the empty dessert road when we came across the canyon. We were speechless with awe. So this was it! We were thrilled. Therefore, it was with disbelief when, continuing on our way for many miles, we came across a huge sign telling us that we were now entering the Grand Canyon, Arizona. We found ourselves with about 16 other people, Mexican, African, Oriental, Caucasian, all moving silently, whispering, mostly just standing there looking into this vast canyon; watching the sun set, blazing flame, purple hues, the sun playing with the clouds casting incredible shades and shadows. We were in Gods cathedral. Our silent exchanged glances confirmed we each knew it. One Negro murmured in passing: "Man! Now I can die happy!" I am not particularly religious. More spiritual.

★

CHILDHOOD EXPERIENCES

How wonderful it would be if we were to listen to our children a little more with our second ear. So many little gems are passed by unrecognised for what they are, but, of course, we are up against vocabulary. We cannot always interpret the content of children's 'stories', especially if our offspring happen to be highly imaginative individuals. We are all familiar with, 'Please God make mummy better', burial ceremonies for dead pets, and so on, but as adults our memories of our own childhood experiences can be uncertain. We have one account from a mother who *did* listen to the implication of her child's chatter. Included here are *OBE*s (out of body experiences).

*OBE*s are not necessarily spiritual experiences, but many who have them view them as such.

(a) *Boy aged ten. I found a dilapidated house near a river and went in climbing up broken-down stairs. Suddenly, in one particular corner I felt an incredible urge to get down on my knees and pray. I returned a few times after this and every time I had the same experience. There was a glow of love and gentleness, which left me gasping. (I was not exactly a gentle child). I kept it to my self. It would have ruined my image.*

(b) *Girl. At all ages, an awareness of unity, particularly with nature – bliss states.*

(c) *Girl aged eight. I had parents who fought a lot. My father was in the air force so we moved around a lot and I was always homesick for wherever we just left. One night I kneeled by the side of my bed and I prayed "Please God, let me know you are there, please be there." I felt something like an electric shock go through me from head to toe (It didn't hurt.) and for that instant I knew, without doubt whatsoever, that there was a God, that he was there for me and that everything was all* right. *I was very happy but kind of stunned because it had been such a powerful experience. As an adult I look back and think, 8 years old!*

(d) *Boy. At the age of seven or eight a dentist placed a gas mask over my face before extracting a tooth. I shot out of my body and observed the operation from the ceiling. I could hear the dentist and his assistant talking to each. I watched the scene, yet I could feel the tooth being wrenched in the body down there at the same time. I never told anybody.*

(e) *Girl aged three. She described floating above the operating table and what the surgeons were saying and doing. Some weeks later when we were going back to hospital to have the bandages removed, she said, 'I can't wait to get all that blue stuff off my hand'. When they removed the dressings, sure enough her skin had been painted with some bright blue substance. There was no way she could have possibly known that.*

(f) When very young this child was afraid of dying. Girl aged five. *I was on holiday with my family in a small cottage in the highlands. I remember I had lost a baby tooth and put it under my pillow to await the tooth fairy. I saw the figure of a young woman dressed in historical type clothes emerge from nowhere, walk through the room. She stopped in front of me, I asked her to go away. (I instinctively knew her name was Maggie.) She did disappear through the l-shaped library I was sleeping in.* After this and other experiences, the little girl felt comforted about ideas of death and dying.

★

MEDITATION

Meditation is included here in a separate section since outcomes are not strictly spontaneous but rather sought by learned techniques, usually paid for. Money does not buy enlightenment, but a high spiritual quotient can find it. In Chapter Four, page 94, we suggest meditation practices might prove significantly more successful in high SQ people, since they will understand that God is found in a self-forgetting, in giving to others – a search path for God quite opposite from an egocentric self-absorption. In recent decades a whole industry has arisen around 'spirit' pursuits, filling the vacuum left by organised religion. They outmanoeuvre the proceeds of anything found in the average church collection box. Picking our way through the maze of recognisable elements of New Age flummery to find meaningful New Age pathways to our better selves demands a balanced approach between an open mind and steady realism. Meditation comes down to us from ancient times, and is being increasingly rediscovered as an effective way to counterbalance the accelerating pace of life in present times. Meditation can be what you want it to be; non-denominational, non-spiritual or simply a way of getting in touch with an inner stillness. Most discover meditation practice brings them closer to the core spiritual self, the essence of being. It can have deeply beneficial effects for both the individual and society. However, as the account of DB/059 illustrates, meditation may not be without inherent dangers.

BH/056/f/*ccm*. Canada. Age thirty-eight

I had just found out I had cancer. During my first guided meditation through music, I experienced an amazing and unexplainable state of being. It was beautiful and I did not want to come back from the place I was. I felt peace and enlightenment; I was seeing a wonderful white light and crashing waves that I can remember. I felt blessed and totally in union with what I was seeing. I felt big and small at the same time. I truly believe that this experience had an impact in my subsequent cancer operation and aggressive treatments. Through it all I knew deep down that I was going to be alright no matter what – and I was.

BH prefers keeping her experience to herself. She was non-religious before and after event.

★

RH/057/m/*ccm*. England. Age twenty-eight

Transcendental Meditation. *The experience is of the mind expanding but not in any way you can explain easily! Thoughts become more irrelevant as the attention is drawn towards a higher state of bliss, consciousness becomes purer, you feel a sense of completeness, it is a state of total relaxation and unboundedness but not tired just wide awake and staring into infinity. The body unwinds and deep stresses are released. There is also a sublime feeling as it reaches parts other techniques don't even acknowledge. Easiest to say that consciousness becomes aware of itself, of its own fundamental nature which is infinite unbounded bliss and deepest intelligence. Sometimes this experience hangs on into daily life and I am to all intents enlightened which is obviously wonderful! But it doesn't render me ineffective at work, quite the opposite, it's hard to imagine a more perfect state of existence, as this would appear to be attainable I conclude it must be the next step in human evolution. Wonderful. It is like seeing the world for the first time, enough to make you cry with happiness. It broadens horizons; more forgiving, aware that life is different for people depending on their state of consciousness.*

RH was not a member of a religious group before or after practising transcendental meditation. Broadcast widely against the advice of his TM teacher but came to understand that: *people don't understand, best to keep it quiet.*

★

EC/058/m/*ccm*. England. Age fifty

My wife died about a year earlier, still very upset. I had been following a guided meditation when suddenly I found myself surrounded my a cloud of white light and heard the words 'I and all my works are all there is.' I experienced a massive outburst of unconditional love, followed by confusion about why God would ever want to talk to me. I have been doing more groups and slowly refocusing my life towards soul-inspired work.

EC told two people; otherwise he kept it to himself.

★

DB/059/m/*ccm*. England. Age forty-six

I was depressed and confused but simultaneously clear about why I felt like that. I was deeply committed to discovering a transcendent reality for myself. I had an intellectual conviction it was possible. It occurred while meditating. But it was nothing like I had anticipated. I realised that my consciousness had slipped beyond its focussed attention. It was a separate 'event' to the activity of the mind. It came of its own accord. It is best described as losing the boundaries of the self, losing the sense of being circumscribed by the body. It was gentle and extremely subtle drift into an emptiness that was paradoxically full. Peace and bliss are words that describe it, but more than that, for me, it was the word Truth that came to mind. Following this: I was very happy and contented. I seemed to have all my questions answered. I was also surprised, but pleasantly so. The state of consciousness has never left, it remains a constant 'presence' although I no longer meditate or practise spiritual disciplines, and it returns often in full-blown form. The event has impacted drastically on all aspects of my life. The experience comes over me automatically at times and life can be a blissful experience. But at other times it can lead to depression and an inability to do anything with enthusiasm. Often I am paranoid and disturbed, though never to an extent that is dangerous. I have only told a few people who I hoped would understand. Most people don't. I certainly don't discuss it among staff at the University. The antipathy to talk of transcendental truth and universality is rigorously opposed.

DB was brought up Roman Catholic. He was not a member of a religious group before or after the event.

★

JS/060/f/*ccm*. England. Age forty-two

Quiet meditational feeling filled by spirit. Started as a feeling of lightness and joyfulness in my arms. Full event felt like a very large bird landing in the middle of a tree (with me as the tree).

No longer felt alone. Befriended and cared for. The experience came about as a result of various changes life changes – breaking addiction to smoking and drinking and resuming meditation techniques. I am hardly fearful for myself anymore. Anxiety and uncertainty is reduced. Shyness dissipated. More confident, happy and genuine, less willing to lie, less ambitious, less angry.

JS was not a member of a religious group before or after the event. JS told two good friends.

★

PKC/061/m/ccm. England. Age twenty-two

I decided to go for a country walk on a crisp spring morning. I took a copy of the Ashtavakra Gita and meditated on the opening text. I found a secluded spot overlooking the Medway river valley, sat down, closed eyes and meditated on the AUM syllable. I had used this meditation before but without any remarkable effect. I meditated for about fifteen to twenty minutes and then stopped and opened my eyes. But I could still hear the AUM sound. AUM was coming from the sky, it was coming from the ground, every leaf of every tree and bush was singing this beautiful vibration. It was overwhelmingly powerful, overwhelmingly peaceful, and overwhelmingly beautiful. At that moment I felt truly blessed. I was in a state of utter peace and contentment. The experience lasted about between thirty to sixty minutes during which time I wandered around the countryside in harmony with everything. This was the voice of God, the song of the angels in the highest of heavens. The AUM vibrations gradually faded and eventually I made my way home and slipped back into normality. This experience was for me my baptism. It proved to me that God exists, that God is within each and every one of us… that we should follow Christ's injunction and seek within.

PKC mentioned it to a few people at the time.

I have never been able to commit myself to a religious organisation.

★

NEAR DEATH EXPERIENCES (3)

NDE is a well-researched phenomenon, records of which can also be found in ancient writings. In modern times NDE research is the first to bridge the credibility gap between science, religion and spirituality, thereby giving greater potency to the question, where lies the boundary of the mind? It is highly suggestive of an encounter in an extra dimensional realm of reality. Travelling through a tunnel towards a vibrant bright light is its most common feature. Often there is choice given whether to return or go on. Sometimes the experiencer is persuaded to return, still others return out of fear of the unknown. All who return are deeply influenced by the NDE; they know there is some form of life after death. As in *peak cosmic consciousness* – divine light, in NDE time and space cease to have meaning; yet paradoxically, interactive thought structures persist as they do in peak *cosmic consciousness* – celestial. Survivors live to tell us their stories, each reflective of the mind of the individual but all identifiably NDEs. Occasionally NDEs are traumatic, frightening and even hellish, but mostly they are rewarding. Near death journeys may enter light, exquisite darkness or scenes of serenity and beauty. Below are examples of the last three. (We may speculate that NDEs mirror the SQ of the individual.)

WP/m/*nde*. Ireland

I was in America in Westminster, Pennsylvania. The visit was both pleasure and business. While in the City Hall I began to feel unwell. I experienced violent pain in my heart. I was taken to hospital and found myself in the I.C.U. Two nurses came to my assistance and administered injections. Immediately I shot out of my body and there on the opposite side of the room stood my maternal grandmother. She smiled at me as she stood beside a tunnel. At the end of the tunnel I could see a bright light, which issued an amazing sense of peace and contentment. Granny 'told' me I was to enter the tunnel, which I did. I knew instinctively that this was the door to the next world. I went down the tunnel but a short distance when I thought of Margaret, my wife and what would she do in America without me. At once I found myself back in my body. It was a profound experience.

★

AB/f/*nde*. England

As I was resting I suddenly felt the bed open beneath me as if it was cut by a knife. I felt myself pushed down below the bed's surface and then entered a tunnel. I heard a rushing noise like the sound of a huge waterfall. I felt myself propelled at great speed through the tunnel emerging out the other end of it into space. Total silence, darkness and nothingness. I heard a voice (a man's voice) speak to me saying, "I am". At this point, my terror overcame me and I found myself travelling back through the tunnel and into my bed, where I woke. It totally changed my life, giving me a wider perspective than I would have had otherwise. It became the foundation of all my searching, my writing and ultimately, the ability to convey to others through my lectures and books the new consciousness that is trying to emerge at the present time.

★

WP/m/*nde*. Ireland

Down in the Intensive Care Unit again… I went out like the proverbial light and there was my tunnel. I went down this at the speed of light and came out the other end. What a staggering sight I saw. No words could be found to describe the scene. It was simply wonderful. I found myself in a beautiful flat land with the most magnificent lawns one could ever hope to see. They were in the form of triangles and circles. All were surrounded by rolling gold which radiated out the Love of God, Peace, Sanctity, Forgiveness; the dictionary could not contain the adjectives necessary to describe what I was experiencing. Away in the distance I could see a magnificent range of blue mountains while from my left a gentle warm breeze came from some sea I could not observe. There were people there – men and women – but I was unable to differentiate between them as they all were dressed in long flowing gowns of beautiful grey silk. They were walking in two's and three's along these staggeringly beautiful paths absorbing all the Heavenly Energy that was being radiated. While standing there in awe a woman approached me (at least I think it was a woman) and said, 'You are not to be here!' I replied, 'I am here and I am staying here!' I argued with her but she kept repeating that I was NOT to be here, that I could not stay in this wonderful place. Then I turned my head to look over my left shoulder and there, about one hundred million miles away I could see a speck of light which was THE EARTH! I could see the cord that was linking my physical body to my spiritual body and came to realise that the 'tunnel' was, in effect, my own Spiritual Cord. From this vast distance I heard a voice which said 'Bill, come back!' 'No I won't' I replied, then, 'But what about your family?'. I replied, 'My family can manage perfectly well without me.' No sooner had I said this when a terrifyingly strong suction took hold of me and with the speed of light I sped back down the tunnel and found myself back in my body. I WAS DISGUSTED!

And, one is tempted to add, so he should be!

★

Perspectives of the Cosmic Conscious Mind

The gift of *cosmic consciousness* is one of unity, freedom from separation between one human being and another: the ultimate imprint of love. Therefore, to turn away from the needs and sorrows of the world in pursuit of an ego-centred ecstasy is the ultimate betrayal of truth.

Survey 2003 shows *cosmic consciousness* has occurred at ages thirteen, fourteen and a seven-year-old, indicating that it has gained a foothold on the evolutionary scale. It cannot now be lost. We might be tempted to assume that it is now widespread. Equally, by taking in the current worldview of the human condition we could be forgiven were we to conclude that there is little evidence to support such an assumption. Certainly the cosmic faculty has had a rough passage surviving the human climate of greed, the lust for power, ignorance, arrogance, bigotry, war, self-inflicted famine... we are truly fearfully and wonderfully made. Were it not for love's myriad expressions we would not have survived on this planet thus far. Love is ever the leaven in the bread. However, we have identified a cosmic dimension to love and it is this dimension in which we are interested here.

What implications are there for an emerging cosmic faculty in a world not yet primed to accept it? For individuals, they are at the traditional targeted end of spiritual jealousy and ascribed sainthood, but there are deeper perils. Cosmic conscious people are at all times creatures of their day and age; a little more spiritually mature than the average Joe, maybe, but not always. There are those who though eminently mature – emotionally, intellectually and spiritually – nevertheless do not access their *cosmic consciousness* within their lifetime. If it were the case that the continuum of spiritual maturity is found independently of the cosmic mind, it naturally follows from this that there will be variable degrees of a spiritual quotient among the cosmic conscious. This begs the question; what, then, is the trigger that brings *cosmic consciousness* into being? We suggest it may quite simply be the presence of suffering and a deep sense of longing to connect with one's soul – the ground of our being – but we do not yet know the answer to this question; certainly it cannot be ascertained from a tiny survey sample.

The magnitude of the *peak* intensity of *cosmic consciousness* is not easily brought into perspective. Questions inevitably spring to the fore: 'am I mad or am I, as Dr Bucke has suggested, part of a race set apart?' The answer is neither. We are not mad and neither are we a race set apart. We are, most assuredly, an integrative part of the whole human race. Because there is little or no access to others having received the same experience and, therefore, little opportunity for dialogue, we are left closeted with our 'secret', not always knowing what to think. We are, therefore, highly vulnerable, at risk, exposed to divine arrogance, proof that we are not saints or a race set apart but fallible humans. Survey 2003 has accounts from people who, exposed to misunderstanding and left in isolation, surrender to that most sorrowful of states, the 'holier than thou' condition.

For those who experience *peak cosmic consciousness* it is sufficient to live through a few seconds of that divine power, a knowing, loving energy, a guiding current of love, which we usually refer to as God. It is enough. Psychologically one is strengthened by it. Its effect lasts a lifetime. However, apart from the 'holier than thou' condition, the power itself is so great it has the potential to unhinge the functioning of the brain. The real problem can arise when the cosmic effect is experienced over long periods, hours or even weeks at a time. One has to be an extremely strong character to absorb protracted cosmic energy. The life of Edith Walters demonstrated the possibilities. She lived in a continuous cosmic condition that enhanced her every day activities and mental alertness. She was an advanced soul well ahead of her time. Even so, there were periods when she withdrew into silences. Since *cosmic consciousness* is neurologically based, there might also be strengthening functions that will evolve to compliment cosmic energy within the workings of the brain. At present our brain is a relatively primitive organ barely equipped to withstand protracted episodes of *cosmic consciousness*, but it has enormous untapped capacity. *Cosmic consciousness* is a newcomer on the evolutionary journey in spite of the fact that we can trace its existence from records written several millennia ago. As Bucke's vision has it, in eons of time human beings will be as different from us as we are from Palaeolithic man.

Meanwhile, there are certain risks inherent. Accounts sent in to Survey 2003 illustrate this. Take the case of 'Brigitte' who whilst driving on a United States freeway became aware of her altered state of consciousness. She realised her car speed had reduced to a crawl and that traffic was whizzing perilously all around her. Her motor functions were impaired, reflexes slow, her thinking mind disconnected from her physical movements but, on one level, she knew she was in a dangerous situation. And in that state she worked the car through the traffic onto the hard shoulder. There she thought she had found a state of equilibrium between her 'lower' and 'higher' consciousness and was able to move off feeling centred and secure. However, she soon discovered she was still disconnected. On reflection, she wondered whether she could have intervened to prevent an accident. She arrived at a shopping mall. Her consciousness had slipped into a different focus. She 'breathed' with joy and well-being. Finding herself in a coffee shop and caught up in an overwhelming flood of love and compassion for the people there, she wanted to tell them about it. She became frightened and focussed her whole will power to lead herself out of the coffee shop before she was carted out by 'men in white coats'. She remembered to attend a pre-arranged formal meeting, sitting through it in a gentle state of blissfulness. She was under the influence of *cosmic consciousness* for around two hours. For the rest of that day she was slightly tired and lethargic.

Several years later, Brigitte was alone for three weeks in a 'haven of peace and solitude… among nature's bounty' when *cosmic consciousness* descended again, more gently but no less joyously. This time she was filled with a tremendous sense of power, an enabling boundless energy. Intellectually enhanced too, she found she could write with complete fluency. During that three week period Brigitte entered an altered state several times, each lasting between a few minutes and several hours.

Since her first experience she had feared she would again find herself among people – or worse, behind the wheel of a car – incapacitated, unable to conduct normal appearances and action. 'A dangerous situation to find oneself in, especially if you live in a "developed" country.' As she points out, there is a real problem when one is so far immersed that individual identity fades, when it may not be possible to exit. In any event artificial breaks from the higher consciousness have a jarring effect on the nervous system. 'There will be periods of disorientation, a physical and mental blurring, an off-centeredness.' Side effects include irritability and depression that usually last a few hours. She realised that potentially there was a real danger of losing control or contact with normal reality, a permanent loss of an ability to return fully to cope with the necessities of daily living. One could lose mental balance and remain in a twilight hypnotic state. Remarkably, Brigitte has learned to exit at will, refocus and recover alignment. She learned the mechanics in the shifts of consciousness, the onset, the dwelling within and the mode of exit. She gained confidence. Now she can remain in balance, in harmony with 'my groundedness in every day living… one must learn how to keep a firm foothold within the soil of Mother Earth, for it is here upon this soil that the "Kingdom within" is inherited and is to be lived… it is only the balanced man who can make *cosmic consciousness* his permanent abode.' (RH/057's account on page 210 shows how life-enhancing *cosmic consciousness* can be when harmonised with our daily existence.)

Brigitte's story is one of successful resolution. Not so for another respondent to Survey 2003. His story is essentially the same as Brigitte's but he found himself more frequently immersed by the onset of cosmic energy. Unhappily, he has become its victim and his writings reflect this. There is a profound sense of detachment from the reality of his world. Far from being empowered he is incapacitated showing all the negative symptoms enumerated by Brigitte, plus the deadly 'holier than thou' syndrome. Sadly, his is an egocentric retreat into *cosmic consciousness* as an end in itself, thus negating the very purpose of not only the cosmic event but why anyone occupies space on this earth, which is to share oneself with others in giving and loving relationships, especially those in need. Such introspection is a real psychological possibility. Obviously this is not how it should be, but is this how it will be during the interim period until the faculty is stabilised within the human race? This is the kind of question that can be answered only by extended research. The brain is a sensitive instrument, having a seemingly unlimited capacity for development, but each of its component parts are required to work in balanced synchronicity, especially so if it is to accommodate the powerful cosmic faculty. As Brigitte observed: 'It is our evolutionary "ripeness", which determines our time of rebirth. Many do not survive it; it is very easy to become unbalanced and to lose ones foothold in the reality of this material world.'

Might we deduce from this that over stimulation of the temporal lobe cortical area, (see Persinger Chapter Four, page 93) in a brain not fully equipped to maximise the enormous potential of the cosmic faculty may pose a serious mental health problem? Were this so, it is unlikely its true source would be properly understood in a society where spirituality is not yet accepted as a natural part of the human psyche. How would psychiatry categorise these ungoverned cosmic episodes? Are they, out of ignorance, loosely grouped with manic-depressive symptoms, perhaps? That *cosmic conscious* people should be subjected to chemotherapy is a horrifying prospect. Throughout this book we have pleaded for an open, unbiased approach within neurology and psychiatry to spiritual matters. How we do need good, focussed research. Recognition of the human condition in all its complexity is foundational for good research. Until the tension between science and religion is eased, we will remain in ignorance about the most important aspect of what it means to be human – our SQ. One of the difficulties, as discussed in part one, is the failure to make a clear distinction between religion and its core spiritual content. In other words, tweaking out our innate spirituality. Indeed, science has yet to concede the existence of a spiritual quotient in the human psyche. We await scientific enlightenment, when free, unprejudiced engagement between science and religion may thrive.

No doubt the 'God Spot', revealed as 'mere' neural activity, will be seized upon by the sceptics fed on a dualistic notion of creation. For others, it will be confirmatory of an intelligent universe, where separateness of its component parts is an illusion. The knowledge that divine love is hard-wired into the human brain has staggering significance. In itself it is the miracle to end all miracles. *Peak cosmic conscious* people know this to be true. They need confirmation only in as much that it will subtly assist in gaining a proper perspective of the *cc* measure. *Cosmic consciousness*, in a fully mature brain, is an incredibly life enhancing power for the good. That we carry this potential at all is highly significant. It cannot be to no purpose.

Given a ground base of emotional and mental stability, the *cosmic conscious* mind will not feel elevated above others, neither is there a notion of being apart or separated from the human condition. The opposite is the case. Separation does not exist. Humanity is poured into us all; *cosmic consciousness* is in touch with the pain and suffering of all that is the worst in our own nature, and by extension, that of our fellow human beings. Compassion resides in our soul for ourselves and for others; 'There but for the grace of God go I.' A wish to escape from the messiness that is life is replaced by a strong urge to become involved. One may be subject to lapses of the *cosmic consciousness* – perhaps for up to years at a time – but it never actually goes away. One's awareness is heightened to the abundance of life, love and joy in others, including those fleeting moments of kindnesses expressed naturally and unconsciously. To the *cosmic conscious* mind everything one looks at appears as the secret workings of the divine. One is reminded of Shakespeare's words: 'All the world a stage and all men and women merely players. They have their exits and their entrances' (*As You Like It*). The world continues in its perilous, fluctuating state of instability, its peoples relatively immature. Is the cosmic faculty running in tandem with the evolving maturity of the human race? It would seem not; there would, surely, be ample evidence of equity between nations, bringing about world economic, political and ecological stability. Plainly we have a long way to go. However, we are survivors and love is a sure route to our survival, and so as we slowly wake up to this fact we will learn its language. There is hope.

Humanity is an infinitesimal part of some grand design (but with plenty of opportunity to ad lib!). For every negative there is a positive. One sees unity and purpose shining through all. We see that the fountain of life is love. Pure love makes no distinction between human and divine love. All love is sacred. For every 'evil' there is a counterbalance of love, for every plunge into suffering, forces are at work for its immediate, future or far distant repair. No human sacrifice or suffering is ever meaningless or wasted. Having experienced timelessness, the *cc* mind sees that the past, present and future are simply the perspective we live by, the means with which we are enabled to live through the adventure that is this miraculous life on earth. The past, present and future assist us in carving out a learning curve for our successors, the future generations, but they are not the ultimate reality. The ultimate reality lies in the now – a timeless, immeasurable now. Einstein's dear friend Besso died a month before he did. Writing to Besso's sister, Einstein had this to say: 'He departed from this strange world a little ahead of me. That means nothing. People like us who believe in physics know that the distinction between past, present and future is only a stubborn, persistent illusion.' *Cosmic conscious* people are not the only ones to have discovered the cosmic code.

★

Data collated by reference to the survey Questionnaire

Gender Ratio: 33 Males, 31 Females

Age when event   Males age between 14–50 years
occurred: Females age between 13–70 years

Adherence to a Religious Belief:

In 'Extended *Cosmic Consciousness*' we see an exception to the rule: one person joined a religious group after the event. All except one of the remaining higher intensity *cc* respondents were not religious before or *after* the event. The lower intensity, 'The Hem of His Garment' three were not allied to a religion before or after the event. Two were religious before and after the event. The 'religious' status of three is not known.

These results indicate that the majority of respondents had moved away from a belief in orthodox religion.

Broadcasting the Experience:

Most respondents attempted to relate their experience to others but were soon discouraged. The overall impression is that of an unknown number of people 'out there' who experience profound spiritual experiences.

Family Line:

Cosmic consciousness: Forty-seven respondents said they were unaware of others in the family having had spiritual experiences. One, who said 'No' nevertheless suspected that many of his family members did. Six did not address the question. Four out of the six who said 'Yes' attributed psychic abilities among family members. One reported an *OBE* in the family.

Respondents' Childhood Experiences:

Seven respondents remember childhood experiences. Two were uncertain.

Respondents Occupations:

The following demonstrate the many walks of life from which respondents came, expressed in terms of occupation:

Construction builder; decor designer for television, film and theatre; property manager; production manager, printing; estate agent; artist, painter illustrator; actor; salesman; professor; mental health nurse; teacher; graphic designer; scientist, physicist; clerical worker; university lecturer; activist in charity work; production specialist; warehouseman; staff nurse; lecturer, mathematics & physics; librarian; tax specialist; bus driver; barrister; adult careers; mortgage broker; office administrator; medical research scientist; writer; university tutor; doctor of medicine; secretary; psychotherapist; lawyer; company director; state registered nurse; social worker.

Atheism and Agnosticism:

Survey 2003 questionnaire did not specifically ask whether people were agnostic or atheist before they received their profound spiritual experience, which is possibly an oversight, though it might have caused confusion. Four respondents were positively atheist prior to their experience and most, in the body of their reports, implied atheist or agnostic views. Poised on an intellectual stepping-stone, atheism is a positive, honest move forward. For many this stance remains unshaken throughout their entire life span, whilst for others this position may become precarious. Unwittingly, the scrupulous honesty and open-mindedness that leads to atheism becomes a standing ground that makes the leap of discovery into *cosmic consciousness* all the more astonishing. Scientific and materialistic as secular societies are, they do provide a climate of intellectual freedom, within which atheism can be embraced freed from the penalties of yesteryear.

★

Chapter Eight

Survey 2003 received, as one might expect, reports of: spiritualism, ghosts, telepathy, astral flying, clairvoyance, precognition, telekinesis, healing powers, auras, voices, visions, angels, astrology, crystal healing, reincarnation and one very interesting report of a capacity to see holographically. Because these phenomena are not yet understood they are commonly referred to as paranormal, supernatural or miraculous.

Non-Sensory Consciousness

In Part One, we presented *cosmic consciousness* as a natural outcome of the spiritual faculty, an inherent faculty found in humans in varying degrees. Donah Zohar identifies this as our SQ, spiritual quotient. Historically, the mystic experience is viewed in supernatural terms. Dr Maurice Bucke has overturned that perspective by placing *cc* into an evolutionary context. It is no longer a supernatural happening. It is no more and no less than an evolving capacity within the human mind to connect with the cosmos. The *cc* is a non-sensory consciousness, a different kind of consciousness where usual consciousness is left way behind. In its peak manifestation – divine light – it is not even a consciousness of the self-consciousness, no duality, only universal oneness. We note with interest that Einstein discovered light and matter to be interchangeable. In the *pcc* – divine light we discover that light (not ordinary light) transcends time and space. David Bohm, physicist, recognised light as the ground of all being. Walter Stace, philosopher, draws attention to the features of *pcc* – divine light as being devoid of ordinary senses: formless, shapeless, soundless, odourless and since light is indescribable, colourless also: a non-sensory consciousness. The opposite of this condition – that is, sensation, images, concepts and their attendant desires, emotions and volitions – he calls a sensory intellectual consciousness. And here lies the difference between the *pcc* – divine light and the so-called paranormal. In para-psychological phenomena there is interaction and projection of mind with the current phenomenon. For example, quoting survey respondents: 'I regularly walked through a flower girl in a pub where I worked'… 'I used to see and talk with a pilgrim girl in the back-bedroom in our home.' – 'I see spirits wherever I go.' So often visions/spirits appear spontaneously, bringing great comfort and consolation, as in the case of a woman who had recently lost her father and had been unable to see him before he died. Busy with her life, she suddenly had a vision of him in her head as she was about to step into her car. The picture was large and full of colour: 'I stopped still and realised for the first time that there is another plane of life.' Later she dreamt of her father in a place that had a special light. Behind him were the two children she had lost whilst in their infancy and she 'knew' that they too were at peace. Another was of a man sitting at the bar in the city in Utrecht, Netherlands, when ghosts of his late father, grandfather and father-in-law appeared. There was a family conversation. Voices were received in his head not through his hearing. They were messages of approval, instruction and love, all meaningful and comforting.

The survey had several similar experiences bringing release of emotion and immeasurable comfort. Should science discover that these experiences were 'mere' projections of the human imagination, the integrity of their meaning would remain in tact. That such comfort is to hand is truly miraculous. In general, respondents to Survey 2003 who see visions or spirits were not allied to a formal spiritualist group and had no previous interest in spiritualism, which is often pursued as a substitute for orthodox religion. It would appear spiritualism is a belief system in its own right.

Stace considers the non-sensory intellectual consciousness is not susceptible to spiritualism. Possibly this has to do with the fact that the cc mind is not conditioned to make contact with the 'after-life'. As AS/03/m/pcc observed: 'Questions like "What is the purpose of life?" or "Is there an after-life?" are not answered because they are not relevant.' That is, during cc ontological questions are fully answered by one's state of being and verbal questions are not to the point. The ensuing knowledge base comes not from an interactive 'sensory' dialogue but is derived from an altogether different source of intelligence. The prime function of cc in all its intensities is to inform of the oneness of creation and to impart an overwhelming knowledge of love. They are non-threatening, comforting experiences. Following such experiences there is a certain lack of curiosity as to how our immortality is realised. The knowledge that it does exist is sufficient. In *The Undiscovered Self* Jung has this to say:

> That religious experiences exists no longer needs proof. But it will always remain doubtful whether what metaphysics and theology call God or gods is the real ground of these experiences.

Religion or any belief system would involve concepts of God or gods but the mystic, the *cc* mind, is more at home with love as an energy within creation, not God as a being but that God is being itself. Mystics are not concerned with metaphysics or theology, so in this respect Jung is right. However, Jung did not make a distinction between the religious and the spiritual, but he did make a distinction between the religion of belief and faith and the religion of knowing and experience. His insight into what he describes as: 'Overwhelming numinosity of the experience' is correct; it is wholly unbounded from metaphysical and theological considerations. He goes on to say:

> Anyone who has had it is seized by it and therefore not in a position to indulge in fruitless metaphysical or epistemological speculation. Absolute certainty brings its own evidence and has no need for anthropomorphic proofs.

The *cc* mind, though not susceptible to spiritualism, is open to other phenomena, which because they are not yet understood are considered paranormal. Out of the sixty-four *cc* accounts, four reported experiences in which voices featured. The voice will be heard as if coming from the room or space one happens to occupy but the knowledge as to its source is that it clearly comes from within oneself but is of something 'other'. It is accompanied by a strong sense of presence. The numinous presence is either a passive recognition or, at other times, a sense of guidance requiring positive action. Here we have a holographic way of seeing. Survey 2003 is privileged to have an example of holographic vision. Just as the survey is able to demonstrate that *pcc* has entered on the evolutionary scale at age fourteen, (and at age seven in the case of David Spangler) our single report of conscious awareness of holographic vision establishes its existence in the human brain.

FP/f/*Holograms*

For as long as I can remember I have seen (I suppose through my third eye) images which appear as holograms. They appear in black and white and can be of people, places, events, etc. each 'looming' up as a moving, single flash frame and usually then disappearing, only to be followed by another. (I don't know if the images are connected). Several years ago I became 'consciously' aware of them and found that I can just turn this on and off (don't ask me how!) at will. However, sometimes these appear spontaneously, usually when I have just woken up and my brain isn't in gear. Most of the time I don't know who the people, etc. are even though they appear with such clarity. Although I don't altogether feel comfortable about relaying the next bit, perhaps it might help illustrate what I see. In August 2001 I was staying with a friend and woke up in their spare room. Immediately, I had a 'spontaneous' image of a plane crashing into a large building followed by a huge conflagration. That was one 'frame'. The next frame seemed exactly the same, except the plane crashing into the building was coming from the left hand side (the first was coming from the right hand side). I was shocked, and thought that there had been a plane crash (it didn't occur to me that there would be two planes and two buildings, although that is exactly what I saw). Then I thought of my brother-in-law who is an airline pilot and yet somehow I knew it wasn't him. I got ready to go to work and stopped off at the paper shop on the way as I was convinced that there had been a terrible air crash. Nothing in the newspapers. I was quite disturbed for a couple of days and then forgot about it. I have told only three people this, as I am not interested in going down the line of making predictions or clairvoyance/psychic stuff.

For FP holograms are natural, and therefore they are not intrusive. The 'frames' are moving images (people talking, smiling, walking, etc.). She is not aware whether images are premonitions or not. In the case of the World Trade Centre the connection was made some days after it had happened. She does not know at what point in space/time the 'frames' that she sees will occur or has occurred/is occurring. She does not become obsessed with matching up 'frames' with 'events'.

HOLOGRAPHIC UNIVERSE

It can be seen that the above account implies information from a collective consciousness relaying intention. Karl Pribram, neurologist, considers the holographic model of the human brain can explain collective consciousness and other phenomena, including premonitions of events such as accidents, that deeply challenge our notion of free will. Were hologram vision to be experienced by most of us, it would be lifted out from the paranormal into normality. The difference between the paranormal and 'normality' is that they are arranged in unfamiliar patterns. One is tempted to say that, like a hologram, some paranormal phenomena are images, ghosts of our reality. (See David Bohm and his holographic model of the universe discussed in Chapter Four.) One significant fact to be noted about the holographic idea is that it occurred simultaneously to two men independently of each other. So often these coincidences precede a break-through in scientific discovery. Bohm, particle physicist and Pribram, neurologist, both distinguished in their respective professions, came to realise how the holographic model accommodates the complexity of the natural world of the mind and of the universe. The two men eventually met to share their ideas.

A hologram, as we recall, (Part One, Chapter Four, page 110) is a photograph taken using a complex process of laser beams to create an interference of criss-cross patterns like waves of water rippling through each other. Laser light is apparently very pure, and so it is ideal for creating interference patterns, which are then recorded on film. The hologram, unlike normal photography, is three-dimensional and can appear eerily life-like. Furthermore, if the film is cut, each piece will record the whole and will go on doing so on ever-smaller cuttings. This is how Pribram came to see how the human memory could work. The holographic model of consciousness makes processes such as perception, imagination and memory explainable. One 'frame' is every frame. Every bit of information stored in our brain is cross-referenced, infinitely so, with every other bit of information, in creative patterns. The whole thing is compounded by the Bohm/Pribram view of holograms interlacing, interacting, retrieving, discarding imagery into infinity, past, present and future melding into oneness throughout the universe; an ever kaleidoscopic holomovement. Bohm preferred the term holomovement, extending this to the whole universe, to counterbalance our familiarity with 'stills' in photography. The universe as a kind of gestalt is an extremely difficult concept to grasp, but if one can accept, on trust, the idea that separation is an illusion, that there is only oneness, it becomes a little easier for us. Pribram considered every atom contains a hologram of the whole. Bohm called this the Implicate Order. 'To see the world in a grain of sand and heaven in a wild flower' (William Blake) takes on a new meaning. Bohm, in his *Wholeness and the Implicate Order*, commenting on Pribram's work on brain structure tells us that:

> Pribram has given evidence backing up his suggestion that memories are generally recorded all over the brain in such a way that information concerning a given object or quality is not stored in a particular cell or localised part of the brain but rather that all the information is enfolded over the whole. This storage resembles a hologram in its function, but its structure is much more complex.

As Edleman pointed out, the human brain is the most sophisticated entity in the known universe and we use a mere fraction of it; sounds, light frequency domains lying dormant to give rise to faculties awaiting the arrival of the evolutionary trail. That stunning prowess exists on earth is manifestly evident in other species; for example, insects that fly at breakneck speed yet see all they need to as they whiz by, a breed of seabird that can skim (walk) on water on its paddles, eagle eyes that see what we cannot close up, sights and sounds invisible to us but which exist in abundance in other creatures. It is not unreasonable to suppose that much of what is now viewed as paranormal has a scientific explanation. If Pribram is right, the truth will be revealed in further research into the brain's evolving capacity.

Jung believed we are beings without borders linked together at some profound level of existence. Take for example dreams; they may not be a primitive substrate of our selves but quite the opposite. Dreams can be a source of learning and enlightenment, but most people hardly pay attention to dream material unless the content is dramatic and vivid, its immediacy rising from the depth of the unconscious. They are unforgettable and unmistakably meaningful. Very often, it would appear, the meaning cannot find a link.

Occasionally, broadcasted tragedies provide the link.

DREAMS – PRECOGNITION

RD/f/dp. Scotland

I was given a photo in my sleep of a group of children aged about 6 or 7 years old with a tall lady. As I looked at the photo they all fell down and were mutilated! I woke up crying and very distressed and woke my husband up with my crying and sobbing.

My mind was very upset to think that I had mutilated children in my mind. This was the early hours of a Monday morning. On the following Wednesday I heard on the radio about Dunblane. It was not until the Thursday when I saw the school photo of children who had been killed that I realised that was the photo I had seen in my sleep. It made me wonder why had I been given prior knowledge of this event.

Dunblane massacre: in the Scottish town of Dunblane a gunman mowed down a class of children leaving sixteen dead with their teacher, on March 14th, 1996. RD had another similar experience the following year.

I woke up crying and sobbing early hours of a Sunday morning August 1997. I told my husband that I had been at a scene of an accident and a young woman in her thirties had been badly injured. As a nurse (State Registered Nurse) I was trying to do cardiac resuscitation but there were pieces in her chest and I couldn't remove the metal. There was a team of doctors and medics around us and they would not do anything to help. They just stood and watched as I screamed at them to help. I was sobbing because I knew the young woman would die. I found out early that morning that Dianna Princess of Wales had been killed in a motor accident.

★

IK/m/dp. Switzerland

I woke up one night at 4 a.m. Unusual for me. I knew it was 4 o'clock because I looked at the clock on the bedside table. I asked myself what it was supposed to be. I went straight back to sleep. Then in a dream, I found myself standing on a nearby pavement of a road, which leads gently to the foot of a local hill. From the left, on the road, (driving on the right in Switzerland) I saw what looked like a coffin on wheels coming towards me. This contraption stopped in front of me and looking down through a glass lid, I saw my step-father lying there. He opened his eyes and then he opened the lid with his left hand, and, sitting up a little, looking well, pink cheeked, he told me he just wanted to let me know how happy and well he was. Nothing more. He lay back, closed the lid and the contraption went off towards the foot of the hill.

I woke up again, it was five minutes past four. I knew Dad was dead. Then I did a silly thing. I didn't wake my wife up. I thought 'Oh it can't be true'. I even went straight back to sleep again. When I woke up, to get up, I thought about waking her but once again I left it. I got my own breakfast, showered and went to work. But I knew it. At about nine o'clock my wife phoned me at work to say that Dad had died, my brother phoned. Dad had died in hospital early that morning. I didn't know he was ill, I didn't know he was in hospital, but I do know that somehow he told me – he was in London and I was in Zurich.

★

PW/f/dp. Wales

My daughter was about 17yrs. One morning she woke extremely distressed. She said she had dreamt that a child had just been killed outside our village Post Office, knocked down by a car. She insisted that it had happened but of course it hadn't. Anyway it was too early in the morning. All day she was in a state of distress, wanting her sisters to go around the village with her to tell people to keep their children away from the Post Office. At first everyone treated her with a mixture of exasperation and indifference but later we became very concerned for her and persuaded her to rest. Next morning the whole village was shocked by an accident outside the Post Office. A little girl, not known to the village had run out in front of a passing car and was killed outright.

★

Carl Gustav Jung:

> The dream is a little hidden door in the innermost and most secret recesses of the soul, opening into that cosmic night which was psyche long before there was ego-consciousness, and which will remain psyche no matter how far ego-consciousness extends.

★

OUT OF BODY EXPERIENCES

DP/m/*obe*. England

This account has the appearance of an *OBE* (out of body experience). Although DP was out of his own body he did in fact occupy a substitute body and was aware of it throughout the whole episode. Experts who study *OBEs* and lucid dreams might see a 'wake initiated lucid dream' (WILD). However, in company with most *OBEs* this recipient says his experience was more real than a dream. Lucid dreamers know without doubt that they are dreaming. The sheer sense of freedom from the constraints of the body led DP to make a profound spiritual connection with the experience and our immortality.

...I was alone in the house. The weather was still cool as it was early spring, so I lit the gas fire and made a cup of tea and settled down in an armchair. I eventually dozed off. There is no denying this but equally, I did wake up and actually sat upright in the chair. Both my feet had gone to sleep, or 'pins and needles', as they say. I began to massage my feet but suddenly, as though a stream of water was flowing up my legs until it reached my thighs, a huge wave of tiredness seemed to strike me and I remember making a moaning sigh as I flopped back into my armchair, except that I didn't. I moved out to my left as my own body went back. I found myself, I would say, about 4 feet from the ground and I was very small and at first thought I had turned into a bat. The reason I say this is because I appeared to be covered in fur. As it happened I found I was wearing a little fur coat and I could stretch my arms wide apart. I was like a little child and had on what looked like a white smock and to my amazement, a pair of little blue boots. At this time I was feeling no fear only wonderment and a tremendous feeling of freedom, like a bird must feel on the wing. I looked like a child but my thoughts were of an adult. When I thought what had happened to my body I was immediately sprung round and could clearly see my body lying in the chair. Now the strange thing is that while gazing at my body I got the most revolting feeling of dislike for it, probably because, as I indicated, I had this most wonderful feeling of complete freedom and had the conviction I could go anywhere. Everything seemed so bright and magnified including the furniture. I remember thinking I will go away now and will never have to die, which shows I was aware that I had not died. If I tried to speak it was as though the words became thoughts and would be acted upon immediately. I moved out of the living room into the hallway but then I had a panic *thought. I remember thinking if I go away perhaps something will take over my body and I tried to shout out, I want to go back, I want to go back but it came out as pure thought. Immediately I was catapulted back towards my body. The next I knew I was trying desperately to open my eyes but it was as though my eyelids were welded together. I would say it was at least a minute before I could open my eyes. I found myself back in my armchair. I should make it clear I never touched alcohol... and the accursed drug culture was practically unknown to my generation. I have read about the Near Death Experience... but I was not even ill in any way... have had vivid dreams and I know this was no dream, it was completely different... believe something like this happens when we die and so it has strengthened my faith.*

★

NF/m/*obe*. England

...Age nineteen when it occurred... my brother and I left a rural pub for home, he by car and I by motorbike (the novelty of having my own transport had not worn off yet) but by different routes. After a while when I had failed to return my father and brother went to find me, separately. Eventually my brother found me in a nettle filled ditch (mercifully not water filled) not far from the pub... I was conscious, but paralysed from the upper chest down, also my left arm was paralysed. He called an ambulance and I was taken to hospital. Nothing extraordinary about that. Except I do have a memory! I asked my brother some years later to verify how he had found me that night. He said he saw me waving my white helmet in the air. This coincides with the visual memory. I have being some twenty feet away and some twenty feet elevated and seeing my

physical self in the ditch and a car arriving from the right of my vision... The feeling I had whilst in this state was one of total knowledge or absolute connection with everything; and for my other self in the ditch, paradoxically one of dispassionate compassion. This, I later discovered was an OBE... It is interesting to note that recent discoveries in Quantum Physics and the zero point energy field mirrors Akasha in Hindu and Buddhist philosophy... There was a long period of recuperation. Gradually, over the years it has come to colour most aspects of my life. For instance, gave up the rural [blood?] sports and became a vegetarian. How can one eat meat when one knows all life is a developing consciousness and ultimately connected to you, yourself. A bit like snacking on your big toe.

★

Dreams, peak cosmic consciousness, near death experience and out of body experience pose fascinating questions for those scientists not bound by ideologies of materialism. Thus far science has studied brain function as a physical correlate of consciousness, as brain waves, but not consciousness per se. As we have noted, all that is changing. Since the advent of quantum physics the influence of the observer on the wave particle duality has led the discipline into conceding the possibility of a Quantum Mind; i.e. quantum coherence in the human brain.

The *pcc* experience demonstrates (to the recipient) how consciousness transcends even the brain. Certainly, NDEs, OBEs and precognition dreams, and indeed precognition in waking states, also point-up this possibility. Quantum physics and neurophysics have a mutual interest in the subject. Progress appears to be dependent upon whether both disciplines can overcome their traditional classical approach by moving into a holistic model of investigation, but at least, now, the big question is out in the open – can consciousness continue to exist in another dimension independent of the brain? As discussed earlier, in quantum physics there is an analogy that mirrors this process. If two particles have been part of the same system, they retain a mysterious connection even when separated in space, defying the speed of light; Einstein's 'spooky action at a distance', which he did not like. The Pribram/Bohm holographic model is suggestive of the same effect; consciousness enfolded in one giant hologram, each particle containing knowledge of all others. In the NDEs the past, present and future is embraced – some go through a life-review during the experience. In the *pcc* experience the past, present and future is 'enfolded' as Bohm might have described it; enfolded in a unitive state, the wholeness of being.

★

The Seventh Sense

The five senses are perfectly understood: sight, smell, hearing, touch and taste. The sixth sense is reasonably understood: intuition or instinctive awareness, sometimes vaguely felt, sometimes strongly felt; e.g. 'knowing' whether one can trust a stranger or not to trust a stranger, an instinctive feeling that someone is behind you though not seen or heard, a feeling something is not quite right, and so on. Beyond this, that extra awareness that is our innate spirituality is scarcely given recognition. Therefore, our seventh sense is unacknowledged.

Ghosts, spirits, healing powers, voices and vision involve an extension of the sensory faculties, touch, hearing, and sight. Clairvoyance, precognition and telepathy appear to be connected with a collective consciousness. Psychokinesis, sometime in the future, might be attributed to the mind connecting with an energy field. (For example, in quantum physics the zero point field is viewed by some to be an ocean of microscopic vibrations in the space between things. If this were proven, all would be connected in an invisible web of extraordinary power. (Ref. Lynne Mc Taggart: *The Field.*) The fact that all these things, and many more phenomena, have been experienced by people over thousands of years, ought to give pause for thought. Because many of these things cannot be explained by standard scientific method, the science establishment has, in the main, ignored them. However, we have reached a point when this is not so easy to do. Alan Wolf, physicist, in a lecture delivered at the Association for the Study of Dreams held in Washington DC in 1987, asserted his belief that the holographic model would ultimately explain the full range of altered state dimensions, and predicted the development of a new discipline, the physics of consciousness. Not all his scientific colleagues embraced the holographic model, and that remains the position today. However, the physics of consciousness did arrive – within two decades. Inevitably, the study of the 'observer' in relation to the particle in the atom will extend to a study of paranormal states, since it is difficult, if not impossible, to place boundaries around the study of consciousness.

Strictly speaking, there is no such thing as the paranormal. There is human imagination and there is human ignorance. We place labels on those things we do not understand. Religions of the world provide ample evidence. What we cannot understand we explain away as figments of a fertile imagination or we say they are the product of a deranged mind, which sometimes they are. In our ignorance we fail to distinguish one from the other. Out of prejudice too we fail to acknowledge our ignorance. Everyone appears to have his or her limitations as to how far credibility can be stretched. Many of us are unable to believe, for example, that a man, after lying stinking in his grave, will rise on the third day. But it is possible to believe Lazarus could have been raised from the depth of depravity (death) to discover his living soul (resurrection). Is it sensible to accept that a virgin will give birth? Since it is medically feasible for a virgin to receive IVF (in vitro fertilisation) one has to make some modern modification. But then, if a virgin is impregnated with an embryo, technically she is no longer a virgin, I guess. Is it believable that Jesus of Nazareth, after his crucifixion, walked among his disciples and ate broiled fish before their very eyes? In other words, many of us cannot accept anything that violates the laws of natural decay and regeneration on our planet. It becomes easier to suspend disbelief where there is room to manoeuvre and to apply common sense to phenomena that may be viewed as powerful projections of the mind. However, we have to accept that the reality of most profound experiences is rarely given the weight deserved. To those who experience them they are real enough.

One day creation will give up a few more of her secrets. When that day arrives, what we currently perceive to be paranormal, supernormal and miracles will cease to exist (probably being replaced by other phenomena yet unknown). They will then be known by their proper names, paving the way for a clearer view of our spirituality, our seventh sense, that gut feeling, a sniff of the unifying whole, an awareness of our selves and of the cosmos, an extra sensitivity possessed by people who are in touch with their 'loving' awareness, i.e. our *cosmic consciousness*.

★

The Agony and a Touch of Ecstasy

Troubled

Survey 2003 is privileged to acknowledge receipt of long dissertations from people who are diagnosed schizophrenic and mentally deranged. Contrary to our cultural expectations they are cogent, insightful and deeply moving. As always, one is left gasping in admiration for the tenacity of the human spirit. Throughout each account one traces the twin threads of humility and compassion compensating for their suffering.

We will have 'Tim' speak for them all. Tim, threatened by persecutory voices that had the power to reduce him to inertia and crippling depression, made friends with them. He came to understand, after much agony and suffering, that they were unhappy and misunderstood. He realised, he said, that they did not know they were dead. His mission was to help them understand this. He became the repository for disembodied souls, aiding their transition out of this worldly dimension. Thus, by channelling his innate compassion, his SQ, Tim took control of his life. The following is a short extract from Tim's life experience after he had 'made friends' with his persecutors.

The situation is that I am in contact with a group of disembodied souls from the generation who fought the Second World War. At first they didn't seem to realise their situation but we got over that. The group is generally 3 girls and 2 men, plus others who have contact with them. One of the girls, – Alison (who says her real name was Caroline) tells me she was hanged; she stabbed a man who tried to molest and hurt her. The stabbing seems to have been important and has imprinted on her thought patterns. She is intelligent. Another one of the girls remembers being an alcoholic and understands my problem, so I try to moderate any drinking with this in mind. She does not like alcoholism. Then there is Syvian, who remembers being a prostitute, she is playful and fun, likable, concerned about her past. All three remember very little from their past – occasionally something reminds, sometimes upsetting.

The two men, one sounding a little older, 40ish, the other younger, mid twenties, quieter and more adventurous respectively. The younger of the two remembers he was a P.O.W, but the details are vague. The group, who see through my eyes as well as their own, can read my mind, pick up any thoughts (which is difficult, as my mind is not always that clean), and access my memories. They can read a book with me. I'll read while Alison dictates to the others but I have to keep a calm mind, as it is a strange experience to get used to. We watch telly, paint and walk together. They like the countryside and optimistic stories. When they first realised the situation of their being spirits they were concerned, what were they supposed to do? What about heaven? Why hadn't they gone there? Where were the other people of their generation? Could I look up reincarnation and related subjects, myth and folklore to try and find some clues? We found some stories and experiences, or beliefs in a spiritual existence in 'Fairy Faith in Celtic Countries' by Evan Wentz, 1911, to see what sense earlier generations may have made of such experiences. We decided it must be natural. One of the girls said people live, then on death enter the spirit world to live for a span and are then reborn. The group have concerns about modern culture, drugs, violence, etc, and wonder what went wrong with the world. They are aware of current events. It's very strange to be in contact with a group of people, when no one else believes such to be possible, that it is delusional etc, so we've been left to try to work things out for ourselves. The group are aware of this, so we search for sympathetic minds. What else can we do? The spiritual people are individuals.

Note: Evan Wentz in *Fairy Faith in Celtic Countries* concludes that 'dismembered spirits' may be a manifestation of inhabitants from a higher reality that only some of us are able to view. He considers accounts are too consistent to be products of insanity, yet too bizarre for conventional explanation.

★

This next account is included because it is totally different, relatively brief, and its content extraordinary in that it contains knowledge of profound depth. It is an account of a single, and the only episode, experienced by this person we shall call Ray. It is possible psychiatry might recognise a schizophrenic episode. Ray, himself does not know what to make of it. Its duration was between five and six days.

I am an extreme agnostic. In June of 1987 I was driving late at night by a remote spot near the Canadian Border in west central Washington State. I had passed this spot before and felt curious about it. From the road about 1/8 mile away was a rising buff of about 300 feet high with a V cut in it with two indents like dried up ponds on both sides of the 'V' bottom. For the first time my curiosity seemed to focus and become fixed on the bluff at a point on the top right of the 'V'. At that point I became involved in a series of strange mental communications that each time made the hair tingle on the back of my neck and head. This continued for the next five or six days – many times with such intensity that I neglected my surroundings and increased to the point where I became very tired and could not prevent them from occurring. I was told that at the 'place' occurred human degradation and injustice to the human spirit but the event was not important. I was told that my new conception of the place now existed partly in my imagination and partly outside of my imagination, and that I was being communicated to because I had 'knowing' or spirit. In response to my attempts to understand, I was told the following:

Spirit is not soul, Not all people possess spirit in sufficient quantity. Humanity cannot be humanity without spirit. Spirit needs humanity to grow or sustain, but not to exist. Humanity needs spirit to remain humanity. Spirit is knowing. It has no dimension and therefore transcends space and physical representation. It has no limits and does grow. An animal can learn but does not have knowing (e.g. painting being perceived and then created). A 'being' contributes to the spirit and knowing increases through beings. The spirit benefits somewhat from being's knowing while he exists, but more so when he ceases to exist. Knowing can also be diminished, and so that is why the 'place' was relevant. The communicator had an involvement with the place. There also exists an 'anti-knowing'. I asked, 'To a being or a spirit?' and was told 'to a being'. I was also told that there was importance to his communicating with me and that others know what I now know. (Whatever that was?) I was also told that beings exist elsewhere in similar form. I was informed that the communicator was an anti-knowing because he seeks/sought existence. He is now part of...?

I was told to practice perceiving that he exists. I had also previously been informed that I was not important: that the knowing was important, and me only because I had knowing. These communications were increasing in frequency and intensity for 5 or 6 days to the point I felt threatened with no control. I had to get rid of them somehow, and I could not stop them. I eventually resorted to calling several religious organizations and finally received a phrase to repeat over and over. 'I affirm and decree that the white fire and violet flame surrounds me and protects me from all evil entities. I surrender my energies to my master guide; Count St. Germaine in the name of Jesus Christ.' It subsided and stopped. I somehow felt that the communicator related to the white fire and violet flame but not to St. Germaine or Jesus Christ.

I also seem to recall but did not record in those notes that all deaths contribute to some sort of vast universal life force that is redistributed for new life somehow. In the first couple of years after, I would get the tingling on the back of my neck when remembering these events, but I never received another communication. I really have no conclusions about this experience, but would be curious to know if you have had similar reports.

Ray has kept this experience to himself. He was age forty-two at the time. He describes himself as an extreme agnostic. Regrettably, it has not been possible to make contact with this respondent to thank him for his unique contribution to Survey 2003.

★

Addendum

Dr Maurice Bucke was the first to acknowledge the humane in the insane and to apply the 'law of love' to the treatment of individuals. As superintendent of the Asylum for the Insane in London, Ontario, in the 1880s, he was the first to discontinue strait jackets and locked padded cells both in Canada and the United Kingdom. Although psychiatric hospitals are now more enlightened, Dr Bucke's inclusion of the 'spiritual well-being' in his patients' treatment plans is not recognised to this day, though his ideas appeared in print. It is not a factor in the professional training manuals of either psychology of psychiatry. He appears to have been completely sidelined by his own profession.

Psychiatrists, according to their personalities, and to a very significant extent their professional diktat, occupy the role of 'high priest', telling patients and each other what is right and what is wrong, what is and isn't real, what is acceptable and what is insane. People labelled schizophrenic, manic depressive or psychiatrically disturbed are, potentially, among the most creative in society as well as the most destructive. Minds that are delicately and sensitively balanced, that slip easily into spiritual disturbances, require special insights. As a social worker I was once privileged to work with a gifted psychiatrist in a hospital. I was invited to participate fully with him in patient consultation and in the treatment plan. Theory, for this psychiatrist, was a background reference to be used or discarded as appropriate. The patient's individuality was sacrosanct. Every patient's 'truth' was recognised and believed, particularly the most psychotic. Spiritual 'distortions' were revered and the integrity of the individual respected. Failure to recognise a spiritual content as a bona fide aspect of humanity is often the root cause of deepened distress that, in all too many cases, results in long-term damage. In that process of recognition of spiritual qualities of compassion, acceptance, humility and so on, they become part of the patient's inner healing process. Important insights can be achieved. The pertinent question to ask here is; is there a missing link in the initial stage of treatment that leads to the precipitous use of a horrendous range of restraints that might otherwise be avoided? It would seem the answer is 'yes' in a significant number of cases.

Survey 2003 mailbag has heartrending accounts of patients' experiences during hospitalisation. Too many patients emerge from treatment stigmatised, labelled shamefully mad, sick or evil. They find their personalities invaded to the core depth of their being; by injections, sleeping pills, anti-depressants, seclusion orders, insulin shock treatment and ECT (electro convulsive therapy). No one knows how ECT really works. This fact alone makes it unethical practice and bad science. Too many people detained under the Mental Health Act, 1983 (UK) do not consent to 'treatment' but get it anyway. It is known that ECT impairs ability to form new memories and is the cause of confusion, among other negative side effects. Some patients claim long-term brain damage from over exposure to electro convulsive therapy. At its core, the psychiatric establishment has still to struggle out of the dark ages.

It would be helpful to acknowledge that psychiatry reflects a society that has yet to grasp a holistic perspective. Where there is ability on the part of the therapist, at the onset of emotional pain, to empathise and fully address the seeds of a spiritual journey which needs acceptance and nurturing, the worst of that pain can be ameliorated. When the present root of the holistic perspective takes a firm hold in society, we can expect a sea change within all its institutions, including psychiatry. A spiritual quotient can then take its place naturally with other human aspects; sexuality, imagination, emotion and so on. Thus far we rely upon the individually gifted psychiatrist with a pioneering vision, of which, thankfully, there appears to be a growing number.

★

Bibliography

Bell, I S, *Speakable and Unspeakable in Quantum Mechanics*, Cambridge University Press, Cambridge, 2002

Bohm, David & Hiley, B J, *The Undivided Universe*, Routledge, London, 1995

Bohm, David, *Wholeness & the Implicate Order,* Routledge & Kegan Paul, London,1980

Bohr, Niels, *On Atoms & Human Knowledge,* Wiley & Sons, New Jersey and Chichester,1958

Bucke, Dr R Maurice, *Cosmic Consciousness*, Penguin Books, New York, 1901

Cairns-Smith, Graham, *Genetic Takeover and the Mineral Origins of Life*, Cambridge University Press, Cambridge, 1982

Capra, Fritjof, *The Tao of Physics*, Wildwood, London, 1975

Cathcart, Brian, *The Fly in the Cathedral (About Atoms the Easy Way),* Viking, Penguin Books, London, 2004

Coles, Robert, *The Spiritual Life of Children*, Houghton Mifflin, Boston, 1990

Dante, *Inferno*, BBC, London,1966

Darwin, Charles, *Descent of Man*, Murray, London, 1871

Darwin, Charles, *Origin of the Species*, Murray, London, 1862

Davies, Paul, *The Mind of God,* Simon & Schuster, New York, 1992

Dawkins, Richard, 'Universal Darwinism' in Bendall, D S (ed.), *Evolution from Molecules to Man*, Cambridge University Press, Cambridge, 1983

—— *The Selfish Gene*, Oxford University Press, Oxford, 1989

de Chardin, Peirre Teilhard, *The Phenomenon of Man*, Harper Bros., New York, 1959

de Chardin, Pierre Teilhard, *Towards the Future*, Collins, London, 1974

Deacon, Terrence, *The Symbolic Species*, Penguin Books, London, 1997

Dennett, Daniel C, *Darwin's Dangerous Idea*, Penguin Books, London, 1995

Dostoyevsky, Feyodor, *The Brothers Karamazov*, The New American Library Inc., USA, 1980

Drexler, Eric, *Engines of Creation (Nanotechnology)*, Anchor Books, Doubleday, USA, 1986

Edelman, Gerald, *Bright Air Brilliant Fire*, Allen Lane, Penguin Books, London, 1992

—— *Neural Darwinism*, Basic Books, New York, 1992

Eliot, T S, *Old Possum's Book of Practical Cats*, Harper Collins, London, 1999

Emerson, Ralph Waldo, *The Over-Soul, Selected Essays*, Penguin Classics, London, 1985

Evans, Eifion, *The Welsh Revival of 1904*, Evangelical Press, Wales, 1969

Feynman, Richard, *What Do You Care What Other People Think?* Bantum, New York, 1992

Gifter, Amanda 'Throwing Einstein for a Loop', *Scientific America*, December 2002

Girardet, Herbert, *Living Lightly Journal*, Issue 20, Summer 2002

Goddard, D, *A Buddhist Bible*, Harrap and Company, London, 1956

Goethe, *The Penguin Poets*, Penguin Books, London, 1972

Hardy, Alister, *The Spiritual Nature of Man*, Oxford University Press, Oxford, 1997

Hay, David, *Exploring Inner Space*, Penguin Books, London, 1982

Heisenburg, W, *Physics and Philosophy, The Revolution in Modern Science*, Penguin Books, New York, 1989

Heschel, Abraham, *God in Search of Man,* Farrar, Straus & Giroux, New York, 1959

Hoyle, Fred & Wickramasinge, Chandra, *Evolution from Space*, Dent, London, 1981

James, William, *The Variety of Religious Experience*, Fontana Press, London, 1971

Jenkins, Rev. David, Bishop of Durham, *Free to Believe*, BBC Books, London, 1991

Jones, Brynmor, *Voices from the Welsh Revival*, Evangelical Press of Wales, Wales, 1995

Jung, Carl Gustav, *Psychological Types*, Routledge & Kegan Paul, London, 1989

—— *Four Archetypes*, Routledge & Kegan Paul, London, 1972

Karolyhazy, F, Frenkel & Lukacs, B, *Quantum Concepts in Space and Time*, Oxford University Press, Oxford, 1989

Krishnamurti, J & Bohm, Dr David, *The Ending of Time*, Harper Collins, London, 1985

Leuba, J,H, *The Psychology of Religious Mysticism*, Kegan Paul, London, 1972

Lockwood, M, *Mind, Brain & Quantum*, Basil Blackwell, Oxford, 1989

Lovelock, J E, *Giaia*, Oxford University Press, Oxford, 1979

Maslow, A, *Religions, Values & Peak Experiences*, Penguin Books, Harmondsworth, 1976

May, Robert M, *Cosmic Consciousness Revisited*, Element Books, Shaftesbury Dorset, 1993

McTaggart, Lyn, *The Field*, Element Books, Shaftesbury Dorset, 2003

Pagels, Elaine, *The Gnostic Gospels*, Penguin Books, London, 1990

Pagels, Hienz R, *The Cosmic Code, Quantum Physics as a Language of Nature*, Michael Joseph, London, 1983

Pasternak, Boris, *Doctor Zhivago*, Fontana Modern Novels, London, 1983

Penrose, Roger, *Shadows of the Mind*, Oxford University Press, Oxford, 1995

—— *Quantum Concepts in Space and Time*, Clarendon Press, Oxford, 1989

—— *The Large, the Small & the Human Mind*, Cambridge University Press, Cambridge, 1997

—— *Emperor's New Mind*, Oxford University Press, Oxford, 1989

Pinker, Stephen, *The Language Instinct*, Morrow, New York, 1994

Ramachandran, V S & Blakeslee, Sandra, *Phantoms in the Brain*, Forth Estate, London, 1998

Richards, Janet Radcliffe, *Human Nature after Darwin*, Routledge, London, 2000

Ridley, Matt, *Genome – Autobiography of the Species in 23 Chapters*, Fourth Estate, London, 1999

Russell, Peter, *The Awakening Earth, The Global Brain,* Revised Edition, Penguin Books, Arkana, 1991

Schrodinger, Erwin, *What is Life*, Cambridge University Press, Cambridge, 1967

Shakespeare, William, *Hamlet*, Cambridge University Press, Cambridge, 1936

Squires, E, *The Cosmic Conscious Mind in the Physical World*, Adam Helger, Bristol, 1990

Stace, Walter T, *The Teachings of the Mystics*, A Mentor Books, The New American Library, New York, 1960

Talbot, Michael, *The Holographic Universe*, Harper Collins, London, 1991

—— *Mysticism and the New Physics*, Penguin Books, Arkana, 1993

Walker, Evan Harris, *The Physics of Consciousness*, Perseus Publishing, Cambridge Massachusetts, 2000

Watts, Alan W, *The Way of Zen*, Penguin Books, Arkana, 1990

Weatherhead, L D, *The Christian Agnostic*, Hodder and Stoughton, London, 1965

Wheeler, J A, *Quantum Theory & Measurement*, Princeton University Press, New Jersey, 1983

Whitman, Walt, *Leaves of Grass*, Holt Rinehart and Winston Inc., USA, 1949

Wilber, Ken, *Quantum Questions Mystical Writings of the World's Greatest Physicists*, Shambhala, Boulder & London, 1984

Zohar, Danah & Marshall, Ian, *Spiritual Intelligence the Ultimate Intelligence*, Bloomsbury, London, 2000

The Gnostic Gospel of Philip
Gnostic Gospel: Hypostasis of the Archons
Gospel of Thomas
The Holy Bible, King James Version:

        Matthew, 1:23, 3:13–17
        Mark; 1:9–11
        Luke; 1:28–35, 3:21–22, 24:39–43
        John; 1:29–33
        Isaiah; 7:14

The Upanishads

SALLIE & JOSEPH TARRIDE
6309 PAMLICO ROAD
FORT WORTH, TEXAS 76116

Printed in the United States
54108LVS00001B/22